STEAM
NORTH WEST

Above and below: 'Black 5' 45156 resting between duties at Rose Grove Shed 01 June 1968.

STEAM
NORTH
WEST

BERNARD MILLS

FONTHILL

Above: 'Black 5' 44802 at Carlisle Citadel looking south in to the night 14 December 1967.

This book is dedicated to the memory of my close friend the late Keith Holt who accompanied me on many of the trips to the North West and assisted in the early stages of the preparation of this book.

Fonthill Media Limited
www.fonthillmedia.com
office@fonthillmedia.com

First published in the United Kingdom 2014

British Library Cataloguing in Publication Data:
A catalogue record for this book is available from the British Library

ISBN 978-1-78155-258-2

Typeset in 10.5pt on 13pt Sabon LT Std
Printed and bound in England

Connect with us

 facebook.com/fonthillmedia   twitter.com/fonthillmedia

Introduction

Let me take you back to the days of my youth. In January 1967 I passed the driving test and purchased my first car, a little three-speed geared 100E Ford Prefect, complete with pneumatic wipers that slowed up as the speed grew and the rain got heavier. The previous year I had gained my first promotion in what was to be a very happy railway career. So at the age of twenty the stage was set for a bit of adventure.

The summer of 1967 was to be the last full summer of steam on British Rail. Having discovered the 100E had been quite capable of being driven to Upwey Bank and other such locations, after the Bournemouth Line Electrification in early July, attention turned to places further away. I suggested to my two close friends Ivor Hocking and the late Keith Holt that we ought to be off to the North West. Take the 100E to Shap was the general idea. Now that was quite an undertaking then, and such expeditions from the far west of Devon were almost unheard of. Shap was some far away place where people like Eric Treacy and Derek Cross (later to become a friend) took pictures. It was a long way, but undaunted we set off.

There was no motorway until just north of Bristol, and on the almost 130 mile journey on the old A38 to reach it, hardly any by-passes, so one had to go through places such as Plympton, Cullompton and Bridgwater. The northern end of the M6 only went as far as Carnforth; beyond lay Milnthorpe traffic lights and the never ending queue on the northbound A6. It was a ten-hour trip to Preston, but to seek out those last days of working steam it was well worth it.

The summer holiday trip of July 1967 which included two, thankfully mostly sunny, summer Saturdays and some good weather in between produced many good pictures, and those precious colour slides taken that week form the basis for this book. There were no mobile phones then, no gen lines and to be honest not all that much information, but we sought out the steam, and discovered locations such as Heysham and the coastal line from Carnforth. We did not have it all our own way, attempts to photograph the Lune Gorge and the Windermere Branch were thwarted by a combination of rain, bad light and late or non-existent trains, but that was all part and parcel of the life of the Railway Photographer—and still is. Yet we found admirable compensation at little known places such as Bolton-le-Sands.

Wind on a year, and those last few months of steam on BR so memorable, last workings here, there and everywhere else. Railtours all over the place, somewhere different to photograph 'Oliver Cromwell' especially if this was combined with one of the last known remaining steam turns. Out of the last ten weekends of Steam on BR, I drove the 100E to the North West on at least six of them, as well as a another two-week holiday to seek out those last remaining pockets, such as the Carnforth to Skipton pick-up goods. Hours spent waiting on the Fleetwood Branch to photograph the Wyre Dock goods, then there was the atmosphere of those three last 'Cathedrals of Steam,' the sheds at Lostock Hall, Rose Grove and Carnforth. As much as I admire and support the railway preservation movement, nothing can really recreate the true aura of the working steam depot: the soot; the dirt; the smoke; and the shafts of light shining on those steam engines we loved so much.

I would normally return to Devon on a long ten-hour or so overnight drive back in the 100E, stopping at Severn Bridge Services at 3 a.m. approx for a large fry-up—the staff even got to know me! Home was reached and a much-needed bed awaited, but only for a few hours as at least I always arranged a late turn of duty on the Monday. That was the way we did it, long hours of driving and hard slog, and it was worth every inch, every penny, every drop of sweat, every moment of the steam locomotive at work. The pictures now are priceless and I hope you will enjoy them and share the memories. Other than the image below and a handful from my collection, the pictures are all my own work.

Below illustrates just how we did it, captured by the late Keith Holt. Ivor Hocking and myself (I am the young twenty-year-old on the left proudly sporting a GWR tie deep in LMS Territory) scale a gate having photographed 44877, seen in the Background, shunting the Private Siding at Giggleswick on 19 July 1968. The washing is on the line, the fields are nice and green, and the steam engine just part of the scene as it had been for so many years. Yet by the time the film came back from processing it was all history.

As I write these words, it is now almost forty-five years since steam ended on British Rail, indeed most who witnessed the age of steam are now looking forward to the monthly arrival of the pension cheque, yet the fascination will never go away. Join me in this book on an imaginary journey from Crewe to Carlisle, following the West Coast Main Line taking a look also at some of the Branch and other connecting lines.

This book does not set out to be a history of the lines and locomotives, it is intended as a pictorial reminder of the last days of steam. I hope you the reader will gain as much pleasure as I did when taking the pictures, enjoying the swan-song of steam in the North West. I have done my best to check for accuracy of dates, locomotives, locations and any other facts drawn to my attention. Any errors will be down to me, and I would be grateful for any spotted to be brought to my attention.

I owe a great deal of thanks to my newly-found friends in the North West for their help with research, locations, train workings, locomotive identities and all manner of questions I have fired at them, especially: Adrian Bradshaw for it was through him this book was born; Peter Cooper for sharing his detailed knowledge especially of the Carnforth area; Ron Herbert for his intricate knowledge of train working and seemingly all things North West; Keith Harper for some expert guidance on Carlisle; Mike Taylor for his unrivalled knowledge of the Rose Grove area and other matters. I must also mention: Phil Prosser for help with the Liverpool and Parkside areas; also Alan Castle, Robert Gregson, Peter Robinson, Steve Andrews, the late Gregory Fox for their help and assistance; and Colin Marsden for all things diesel. To combine all their knowledge and experience in to one volume has been a privilege, hopefully it is now recorded for the benefit of future generations. Keith Holt, who sadly passed away during the preparation of this book and to whom it is dedicated for providing much information from his notebooks and corresponding pictures; his son Alistair for entrusting me with the precious note books after Keith's death; Roger Geach for helping me to find some of the locations after not seeing them for over forty years, also for help with locomotive history and slide scanning. Barry Jones for imparting his considerable knowledge of computing procedures and software skills, I now know about 'fonts' for example! I must also mention Helen Henderson for help with all things flora and fauna, Garry Baird for production of the map, my drinking companions John Lane and Jeremy Clark for proof reading. So many good people have helped and assisted in the production of this book, if I have missed anyone out I apologise. Then there were those steam engines battling over the Fells, and the Crews who manned them, they will remain forever in the memory.

Should you wish to enjoy looking at these pictures on your own screen in your living room or by means of a nice large size print, these are available through the Classic Traction website where many more of my pictures can be found at:

www.classictractionimages.weebly.com
or alternatively visit
www.stores.ebay.co.uk/Transport-Photograph-Archive
where many of my other views including lost lines and stations can be purchased.

For those not familiar with railway operating terms and the four character head code system used in this book, a few very basic notes put in layman's terms to assist. An 'up' train is one travelling in the direction of, but not necessarily to London. Similarly a 'down' train is one travelling in the direction away, but not necessarily, from London. Introduced in June 1960 and still in use to the present day, the four-character head code is used to identify each train. The first number is the class of train followed by a letter which represents a destination area, followed by the two numbers to complete the head code. Very basically to explain those used in connection this book, Class 1 is express passenger or newspaper train, Class 2 is stopping passenger, Class 3 parcels, fish, fruit etc. also empty coaching stock, Class 4 to 9 are various types of freight train. The number 0 indicates a light engine. Thus 1S40 is the 0825 Morecambe-Glasgow, and is a down train but has not come from London. The letter 'S' indicates it is heading for Scotland. 3P04 is the 0930 Manchester Victoria to Blackpool North Parcels, the letter 'P' used to indicate in this part of the world the train is heading toward or within the Preston division. Some of the other letters relevant are 'L' heading for the Carlisle area, 'M' is a train going to the London Midland Region thus the 1326 Glasgow to Morecambe is 1M32, and is an up train heading in the direction towards but not reaching London. The letter 'T' indicates the train is a special working within the London Midland Region whilst 'Z' denotes an inter-regional special or excursion train. The head code has no relevance to the train being an up or down service, I hope this basic simple guide will be useful.

Bernard Mills

On a gate at Giggleswick by the goods siding. To the left the then much younger author, to the right, my close friend and mentor Ivor Hocking. Cameras to the fore, mine a Praktica IV Single Lens Reflex (a bit of a novelty and state of the art then) and I used 64 ASA Ektachrome Film processed locally near Liskeard. Behind the intrepid photographers, the washing is out, 44877 waits to pull out of the Yard, just part of the everyday scene, but it was a scene that would disappear for ever, even before the film came back from the processors. Picture by the late Keith Holt, 19 July 1968.

Abbreviations used in this book

BR	British Rail
DMU	Diesel Multiple Unit
GWR	Great Western Railway
LMS	London, Midland & Scottish Railway
LMR	London Midland Region (British Railways)
LNER	London & North Eastern Railway.
LNWR	London & North Western Railway
L & Y	Lancashire & Yorkshire Railway
RCTS	Railway Correspondence & Travel Society

Crewe to Carlisle

Crewe: Our journey commences at one of the most historic and famous railway junctions in the World, Crewe Station (opened 4 July 1837.) Whilst changing trains there on my way to Scotland I was pleasantly surprised to find 3F 'Jinty' 47521 still engaged as station pilot, by then almost all such duties at major stations had been placed in the hands of diesel shunters. Crewe had several of these 0-6-0 tanks engines as pilots, constantly at work attaching, detaching and shifting vehicles between trains. 47521 did not have long to go being transferred to Stoke the following month and withdrawn from there in September of the same year. 20 June 1966.

Liverpool Speke Hall Road: An industrial setting which is still very similar today. The view looking east from the Speke Hall road over bridge taken the same day as the above picture. '8F' 48356 heads west with a loaded coal train on the slow running line, indicating it is going 'straight on' at Speke Junction a mile or so ahead, towards Garston Docks. At the time Garston Docks had four huge coal drops where coal could be loaded straight from the wagon down a chute into a ships hold. All this traffic and activity is now a part of history. 30 March 1968.

Left above: Crewe: In the evening sunshine, an unidentified 'Black 5' rolls in off the Manchester line with a lengthy freight, and an electric multiple unit awaits its next stopping service back to Manchester. Crewe was a fascinating place in this era to observe the railway at work especially with steam traction still appearing under the electric wires which had arrived six years previously. It would not be very long before steam was a memory here. 20 June 1966.

Left below: Ditton Junction: A slight diversion off our route for a couple of pictures on the line to Liverpool. '8F' 48745 heads west though Ditton Junction station with a coal train on Grand National Day in March 1968. The station, refurbished for the January 1962 electrification of the route, looked rather deserted, most of Merseyside no doubt heading for Aintree. This was the first station to be closed under the privatisation of British Rail, being closed by Railtrack as from 29 May 1994. 30 March 1968.

Above: **Wigan North Western: Of the 842 'Black 5s' which were built only four were named in the pre-preservation era.** 45154 *Lanarkshire Yeomanry* stands at a rather run down looking Wigan North Western station, and about to head south with 1T54 the RCTS 'South Lancashire Rail Tour.' I travelled on the train, and seem to recall it lost a lot of time and ran rather late, traversing the Horwich Branch in the dark. 24 September 1966.

A good place to cross the road and have a look at the line to Southport.

Burscough Junction: After a grand trip around Lancashire with a slight foray into Yorkshire, we catch up with 70013 working the 1T40 Rail Tour in the evening sunshine at Burscough Junction, pronounced 'Burs/co Junction.' The train is coming off the North curve from the Preston-Ormskirk-Liverpool line to join the Wigan-Southport line. Less than a year after the picture was taken, the North curve was taken out of use in May 1969 and lifted in 1973. The South curve to the right was singled in 1970 and survived for MOD Traffic until 1982 and was lifted soon after. Burscough is thus no longer a junction; the formation of both curves remains intact and both routes survive for passenger traffic but are not now connected at this point. 21 July 1968.

Left below: Parbold: With only a couple of weeks to go before the end of steam; a very pleasant picture of 'Britannia' 70013 *Oliver Cromwell* climbing away from Parbold through the houses towards Wigan with 1T40, a special train run by the Roch Valley Railway Society. The purpose of this tour was to run Manchester-Southport four ways with steam; a remarkable achievement then let alone now. We shall catch up with this train in the next couple of pictures and see it again later at Copy Pit. The little 100E did a lot of miles that day. 21 July 1968.

Bescar Lane: 'Black 5' 45110 took over from 70013 at Southport Chapel Street to work the final leg of this impressive rail tour; this part of the itinerary being around the south curve at Burscough Junction and then the former Cheshire Lines Committee route to Manchester Central. One thinks of Lancashire as being of industrial towns, hills and valleys, but to the east of Southport the ground is very flat as is evident in this rather rural view of the train approaching Bescar Lane. Despite the lack of any gradient here, the engine is going well and makes an impressive sight as its smoke rises into the evening sky. 21 July 1968.

Newton Heath Shed: The interior on the second day of a weekend spent touring various locomotive sheds in the North West finishing in the Manchester area. Given the right conditions such places were real Cathedrals of steam where engines rested in an aura of light and shade, just like 'Black 5s' 44735 and 45310 as seen above. The latter had actually brought me in to Manchester very early the previous morning on the last steam working out of Leeds (as we shall see elsewhere in this volume.) Just six weeks later on 29 June 1968 the shed closed to the old order; here no more would sun and shadow fall on resting steam. 19 May 1968.

Left below: Bescar Lane: The going away shot from the above view, 45110 powering through the wayside and somewhat remote Bescar Lane station showing the cottage style construction and the BR 'Totem' signs are clearly visible. The line ahead leading to New Lane is absolutely straight and level here, and when the Lancashire and Yorkshire Railway took over the original Manchester and Southport Company, this point became the lowest part of the L & Y system at just 12.5 feet above sea level. 21 July 1968.

We will now also head for Manchester for a quick shed visit before heading north.

Above: Newton Heath Shed: An exterior view on the same day. To the left a Class 24 diesel stands outside the fairly new shed constructed mainly to look after DMUs. In the centre a Cravens built unit looks rather incongruous stabled amidst the lines of mainly 'Black 5s' with 44949 prominent. Today the site is a major DMU Maintenance Depot for Northern Rail. The depot has also left another lasting legacy: the Newton Heath Lancashire & Yorkshire Railway Football Club was established by the Carriage & Wagon Department of the depot in 1878, by 1892 it had become independent of the railway and joined the Football League. The name was changed to Manchester United Football Club in 1902; the rest they say is history. 19 May 1968.

Bolton Shed: Another of the locomotive sheds visited on the same trip was the former L & Y Shed at Bolton. A good number of engines, mostly 'Black 5s' with 45104 facing outwards, are stabled on a peaceful Saturday afternoon and with Class 08 diesel shunter D3844 on the left for company. The impressive Beehive Mill in the background provides a typical Lancashire Industrial setting. The shed closed on 29 June 1968 and today the site is used for housing. Beehive Mill has fared better, built in 1895 and once the largest spinning mills in the world, it is now Grade II listed and is still in use as a distribution centre. 18 May 1968.

Left below: Trafford Park Shed: The locomotive shed at Trafford Park closed to working steam on 4 March 1968. By the time of my visit it was only used for storing withdrawn locomotives. In the shadow of the nearby Old Trafford Stadium, and with a neat row of lampposts to the left and water cranes to the right, lines of 'Black 5s' await that final fateful journey to the scrap yard. A rusty brazier to the right had no doubt once kept many hands warm and water for the cranes from freezing. Silent and cold it also lays in wait for the scrap merchant. There is no longer any hustle and bustle here. Today the site is occupied by the City Park Business Village and the A56 Bridgewater Way. 19 May 1968.

Blackrod (1): North of Bolton is Blackrod, the station is still open and was once the Junction for Horwich. Heading south towards Manchester, 'Britannia' 70013 *Oliver Cromwell* speeds through with British Rail Scottish Region Grand Tour No 5. To the right of the locomotive are the remains of the goods yard, and the rather fine goods shed which remains standing today and in use as small industrial units. The wooden footbridges across the goods yard and between the platforms were a relic from L & Y days. Removed in the 1970s, the metal bridge that replaced them has itself been superseded by a ramped access to the platforms. Another point of interest is the signal, the Blackrod Junction up starter with the splitting distant signals for Horwich Fork Junction, the latter signal box closing on 14 September 1969. Blackrod Junction Signal Box, obscured by the station footbridge, survived as an interface between the Manchester and Preston Power Signal Boxes until it was abolished on 10 February 2013 and demolished over the weekend of 1-2 June 2013. Within a couple of years the whole scene will alter again with electrification of the Manchester-Preston route. A few notes about the train would not go amiss: leaving Edinburgh at 0755 behind D1773, 70013 took over at Carnforth for the leg to Guide Bridge where E26052 took the train over the Woodhead route to Sheffield Victoria and back; at Guide Bridge 70013 took over again for the run via Blackburn to Hellifield where D1773 was waiting for the return to Scotland via Settle before being replaced by D257 at Stirling, and arrived back in Edinburgh at 2244. The fare for this feast of rail travel was 70 shillings, or £3.50 if one paid the same amount of money today. The current price in 2013 for an off peak return from Edinburgh to Manchester is £70.20.

For more information on Blackrod Station, those with internet access are invited to visit www.blackrod.org.uk. 1 June 1968.

Blackrod (2): Those aboard the Scottish Region Grand Tour No. 5 would have been totally unaware of the helpful London Midland Region sign on the goods yard footbridge, directing prospective passengers for the main line platforms to Preston and Blackpool to the left. Rather more optimistic is the indication to the right for trains to Horwich since the Branch had closed to passengers when the last train departed almost three years earlier on 25 September 1965. One wonders if any unsuspecting passengers took the advice on offer. 1 June 1968.

Lostock Hall (2): This is how steam sheds will be remembered. It is where the engines came to be maintained by 'Men of Steam' who possessed a whole host of arts, skills and crafts and a real pride in the job. Places like this were also dirty, dusty and smoky and there was soot and ash everywhere, the smell could cling to one long after leaving a depot like this. Wonderful, it was an experience not to be missed if one had the chance. '8F' 48666 awaits its next turn of duty as does 'Black 5' 44950 on the opposite road. There is little indication all this would be a memory within three months of taking the picture. 18 May 1968.

Left above: Blackrod (3): Passengers no more. Had anyone found their way to the former branch platform, they would have found this delightful railway byway scene. Not only were the steam engines disappearing at an alarming rate in the period under review in this book; so were many branch and secondary lines, most due to the effects of the Beeching Axe, but that is another story. The short platform for the Horwich Branch was still intact though looking a little untidy. The wooden waiting shelter had obviously seen better days and I wonder how many fond farewells were bid under its little awning. The track continued to serve the former L & Y Horwich Works until its closure in 1983. Curiously, the Horwich Branch does not have an official closing date, the works connection was removed in 1989, and it was not officially demolished, falling victim to metal thieves over a period of time. Sadly metal theft is nothing new. For more information on the branch visit the Horwich Station website. 1 June 1968.

Left below: Lostock Hall (1): Just to the south of Preston and a stone's throw off the West Coast Main line by Farington Junction one can find Lostock Hall and the site of its former locomotive depot, one of the last three to retain steam until the end came at the beginning of August 1968. A general view on what was the first port of call on a Plymouth Railway Circle two day visit to various North West locomotive sheds; the area as we shall see later in this book was reached by a historic journey via Leeds quite literally in the middle of the night. A typical line up and plenty of activity, but note again how the new order of motive power has crept in. 18 May 1968.

24

Right: Preston: The station clock to the right shows it is 1205, so 'Black 5' 44709 is running a little late with 3P04 0930 Manchester Victoria to Blackpool North parcels, booked away from here at 1151. This was a diagram for a Carnforth based engine starting with 1J05 0625 Heysham Harbour to Manchester Victoria, the legendary 'Belfast Boat Express,' then 3P04 and return with 3J06 1350 Blackpool North to Manchester Victoria, finishing with the return boat train 1P02 2055 Manchester Victoria to Heysham Harbour. Not a bad day's work for a steam engine. With the exception of overhead wires and gantries and a few yellow lines on the platforms, a picture taken today from the same viewpoint, the station footbridge at Preston, would look very similar. Note also the little 'tug' vehicle for pulling the station trolleys, the amount of mail on the platform and the fine array of British Railways type signs, all of which have vanished to be replaced by the more corporate image of today's privatised railway. October 1967.

Left above: Lostock Hall (3): The transition from steam to diesel is well under way as a fairly new Class 50 Diesel number D414 takes its place amongst the old order, the class was still under construction at the time and photographs of them alongside working steam are not that common. The Diesel had been leant to the depot for crew training purposes as men had to be taught new skills and a very different working environment to steam. It was indeed a great period of change. With all its soot, dirt and grime a working steam shed was possibly not the ideal place for a brand new main line express diesel, it would not last clean and shiny for very long!

We will return to Lostock Hall later in this volume in a special chapter devoted to the end of steam in August 1968. 18 May 1968.

Left below: Farington Curve Junction: On the outskirts of Preston 'Black 5' 44897 comes off the East Lancashire line to join the West Coast Main Line at Farington Curve Junction with northbound coal empties. The bridge in the background is Bee Lane and just beyond is Farington Curve Junction Signal Box which had a 30 lever frame. In the foreground is the colour light home signal for Skew Bridge Signal Box. The area has been controlled by the Preston Power Box since November 1972. 6 June 1968.

Huncoat: How many generations of small boys have gathered by the line side to watch the trains go by? These young lads are getting a last glimpse of steam here at Huncoat on the penultimate weekend of steam. Running very late (as did everything else that day) 'Black 5s' 44874 and 45017 double head 1Z79 Stephenson Locomotive Society 'Farewell to Steam Tour No. 2' pass the former power station, on a very circular route from Manchester Victoria to Stockport via Diggle, Copy Pit and Rainhill. The power station sidings are well stocked with wagons. 4 August 1968

Left above: Preston East Lancashire side: My only shot of the former East Lancashire platforms at Preston, taken on a dreary day in July 1968 with 'Black 5' 44743 simmering away. A Derby Lightweight DMU stands to the right awaiting its next turn of duty. The former Lancashire and Yorkshire Platforms were in effect a separate station alongside the ex-London & North Western station but numbered as part of the overall sequence. Each side maintained its own buffet, booking office and goods facilities. The East Lancashire side was closed completely in 1972 as part of the Preston re-signalling scheme and today is a car park for the Fishergate Centre. No trace of it remains. July 1968.

Left below: Rishton: A diversion now from Preston to have a look at the East Lancashire system. '8F' 48191 is seen in the rather attractive and rarely photographed setting of passing between the two reservoirs at Rishton with Whitebirk and Blackburn in the background. The train consists of coal empties from Fleetwood Wyre Dock to Burnley Bank Top Sidings, easily recognisable by the 21-ton two-door wagons that could only be accommodated at the Fleetwood Power Station tippler. 06 June 1968.

Huncoat Power Station Exchange Sidings (2): Although adjacent to the former Huncoat Colliery, the colliery alone was not sufficient for the needs of the power station. Much coal was also delivered by rail, thus the need for the exchange sidings seen here looking west with a good supply of National Coal Board wagons behind. Once the boiler was filled with steam, the engine took its wagons up to the neck by the level crossing seen on the previous page and loaded them one by one into the tippler, which took the coal by conveyor over the BR line to the power station boilers. Huncoat Power Station closed in 1984, the two 0-4-0 Bagnalls were scrapped in 1986, the cooling towers demolished in 1988 and the surface buildings had gone by 1990. Mature trees now occupy the site. 20 July 1968.

Left above: Huncoat Power Station level crossing: A charming scene where the already closed (February 1968) line from Huncoat Colliery to the power station crossed the Altham to Huncoat road. One of the power station's fireless Bagnall engines can be seen by the power station fence within the complex. The road is still here, but much wider now, with no sign that a railway level crossing ever existed here. The power station as we shall see is also a memory. 20 July 1968

Left below: Huncoat Power Station Exchange Sidings (1): A couple of views of the industrial fireless engines once employed here. With the main line in the foreground, 'Huncoat No. 1' built by W. G. Bagnall in 1951 (works no. 2989) for Huncoat Power Station (which opened the following year) is taking a breather between its shunting duties. The sidings are well stocked with loaded wagons of coal to keep the little engine busy. Behind are the cooling towers of Padiham Power Station which closed in 1993; the site now is mainly a technology park. Pendle Hill looms in the far distance. 20 July 1968.

Rose Grove Shed (1): A striking head-on portrait of 'Black 5' 45350 at rest on Rose Grove Shed proudly displaying its '10F' shed plate. There is little evidence here of it being just two weeks before the end of steam. One can only surmise how many more years 45350 could have carried on working, there looks plenty of life yet in the then thirty-one-year-old engine. The shed closed to steam as from 4 August 1968, diesels ceased to use the facility in 1971 and it was demolished in 1973. Today the site has mostly been obliterated under the M65 motorway. 20 July 1968.

Rose Grove Shed (2): Rose Grove was one of the last three sheds to retain steam until it closed on 4 August 1968. Just two weeks to go, a busy looking scene as '8F' 48062 is being turned on the turntable, behind and to the left of the leading locomotive on the row of engines is 48393. Note the track to the right full of ash and to the far right the water crane. This is what steam sheds were all about, now it is all gone. If one were able to update the exact scene today, one would be standing on the M65 motorway which would not really be a wise move! 20 July 1968.

Left above: Gypsy Bridge: A popular working with railway enthusiasts right up to the end of steam was the Saturday 3J83 1325 Colne to Manchester Red Bank empty newspaper vans. Perhaps well ahead of his time in paying attention to global warming, instead of the usual Standard Class 5 for the duty, the foreman at Rose Grove Shed was persuaded to turn out a very smart looking '8F' 48257 complete with snow plough, a little out of place on a warm June day! The train is seen here heading west from Rose Grove at the now demolished Gypsy Bridge. The former Rose Grove Shed (which we are about to visit) can be seen in the background with its coaling stage, a once prominent landmark, and the newly constructed road bridge over the station and yards. A very different scene today. The new bridge to join the M65 motorway is roughly situated where 48257 is seen in the picture. Growth and the motorway itself have since taken over the scene, and it is not possible to now take a corresponding photograph. 1 June 1968.

Rose Grove Shed (5): A view of '8F' 48247 outside the shed, showing the inspection pits as well as the oil, grease and water; all of which were of course a staple part of the steam locomotive shed environment. One can only wonder what the Health and Safety brigade of today would make of it all. The, then new, road bridge over the station and yards can be seen in the background, the only thing remaining in the picture today. 20 July 1968.

Left above: Rose Grove Shed (3): A close up view of 48393 and one of her sisters on Rose Grove Shed with coal and dust everywhere, wonderful for the enthusiasts, not so good as a work place. One of the reasons given why BR was in such a hurry to change from steam to diesel was the recruitment problem in getting men to work in such sooty and smoky conditions for what was a low wage at the time. £7 a week to work in coal and ash like this was not a great attraction to the average worker getting used to the trappings of the late 1960s. No Health and Safety rules then, I am sure today some pen-pusher would have insisted on a fence around the turntable to stop anyone falling into the pit. How times have changed. 20 July 1968.

Left below: Rose Grove Shed (4): A peep inside Rose Grove Shed to sample the atmosphere of the place and witness steam at rest. 'Black 5' 45350 to the right and '8F' 48519 to the left are two of the occupants that day awaiting the next call of duty. Note the well-constructed smoke flues which of course are in perfect position to aid the removal of smoke and steam. Soon the engines would go outside the shed forever. 20 July 1968.

Copy Pit (1): Not too far to the east of Rose Grove is the Copy Pit line where we catch up again with 70013 and the 1T40 special from Southport seen previously at Parbold, from where it has been routed via Manchester Victoria, Cheetham Hill, Rochdale and Todmorden and is seen here climbing Copy Pit just to the west of Dean Farm. It is a hot summer's day thus there is not much exhaust coming out from the 'Britannia' but, believe me, she is working hard on the 1 in 80 gradient. The Copy Pit Line has scenery to match both the West Coast and Settle and Carlisle lines, and like the latter not always seen in light like this! 21 July 1968.

Left above: Rose Grove Shed (6): Not all the engines on shed that day were to make it intact to the very end. Beyond the turntable nearest the camera is a sorry looking '8F' 48081 which had been withdrawn on 23 March 1968, one of her unidentified sisters has also been banished to the scrap line. The houses in the background to the right once had a fine view of the shed and its goings on, now they have foliage and the M65 to look at instead. 20 July 1968.

Left below: Rose Grove Shed (7): We sign off our look at Rose Grove Shed with a view of Standard Class 4 no. 75019 just by the coaling stage. This engine was kept in good condition for working the former Grassington Branch to Rylestone Quarry, a line which managed to elude my camera until steam made its last call on these duties in mid-June of 1968. Curiously, the 'Standard 4s' at Rose Grove did not form part of the shed allocation but were out-stationed from Carnforth Shed. The class had been introduced in 1951 and could have lasted for many more years yet they would be extinct by 1968. Seventeen years of working life, what a waste. 1 June 1968.

Copy Pit (2): I have included the going away shot to show how lovely the scenery is here, a real train in the countryside shot. I think this line tends to be overshadowed by the other trans-Pennine routes, it well worth exploring even today. The view is looking towards Copy Pit summit and Burnley. 70013 will proceed via Blackburn and Lostock Hall to join the Wigan-Southport line at Burscough Junction, where as previously seen I photographed the train again. A rather fast run across Lancashire in the little 100E and, of course, we did not have the road system of today. It was all good fun. 21 July 1968.

Lydgate Viaduct: The classic setting of Lydgate Viaduct near Todmorden, and the morning mist is just clearing as 70013 *Oliver Cromwell* forges ahead with the RCTS 'Dalesman No. 2' Railtour. The special train originated in Leeds behind D7568. The pacific took over at Stansfield Hall Junction and worked the train as seen here via the Copy Pit line, Accrington and Preston to Carnforth; thence to Skipton via the 'Little' North Western line which we shall examine shortly, and catch up with this train again at High Bentham and Clapham. Another long Sunday of driving around the North West after steam, but I was not the only one on the case. My good friend Michael Taylor (who has contributed greatly to this book with his knowledge of the Rose Grove area) tells me, '*16 June was a Sunday. I usually worked Saturdays so did not see most rail tours, but went to town with this one. I chased it in my dad's Austin Wolseley 1600 with my wife to be, and my friend Dennis with his girlfriend in the back. We started at Stansfield Hall Junction, then photographed the train just before the summit, chased it to Gannow Junction, Burnley, where we just beat it. I later learnt that 70013 reached 30 mph at the summit from a standing start and 63 mph coming down the bank to Gannow Junction, so I must have had the accelerator on the floor, mind you it was a powerful car. I managed further shots at Wennington and Clapham later in the day.*' Given the chance, would we do it all again? A resounding 'yes' would be the answer! 16 June 1968.

Above: Copy Pit line, Portsmouth Distant Signal: The broad side view from the hill opposite Lydgate Viaduct as 70013 attacks the bank towards Copy Pit passing the distant signal for the former Portsmouth Signal Box. The morning mist has lifted sufficient to reveal how the hills rise steeply behind the train. Here the gradient is 1 in 65, and the engine is going well after a standing start at the bank. 16 June 1968.

Preston: Steam in the night (1): We return back to Preston and there is nothing quite like the atmosphere of steam in the night, finely illustrated by 'Black 5' 44878 standing at what was then Platform 5. The train is 1P58 2048 to Blackpool South, formed from the rear portion off 1L79 1705 Euston-Carlisle, and was one of the last passenger steam diagrams lasting right up to the end of steam. 44878 was not popular with the Lostock Hall crews and had a reputation for rough riding. 30 March 1968.

Left below: Copy Pit Line climbing towards Portsmouth: A dramatic view of steam in the Pennine landscape looking west from Lydgate as the train climbs the 1 in 65 gradient towards Portsmouth. This is the other Portsmouth, not quite so well known as its more famous namesake on the South Coast. No HMS *Victory* here; just the victory of men battling with steam over the gradients, often in the Pennine wind and rain. Interesting though to note this Portsmouth, which lost its station in July 1958, has shifted between counties; it was in Lancashire, before being moved into the West Riding of Yorkshire in the late 1880s, and then in the 1974 re-organisation to became part of West Yorkshire. Whatever the county, it is a lovely part of the world. 16 June 1968.

Preston Steam in the night (4). With 43106 not about to immediately move, plenty of time for once to enjoy night photography at all angles, this is the 'going away' shot with the town streets behind showing up nicely. In these pre-digital days, night photography was a bit of a challenge: using 64 ASA film as here, it was a case of try it and see; there was no yardstick for working out the exposure, one went on a general rule of thumb of about a minute at F5.6 or 8 depending on what light was or was not available. The minute at 5.6 has worked here. The engine is now preserved on the Severn Valley Railway. 30 March 1968.

Left above: Preston Steam in the night (2): More dramatic night lighting for Ivatt 'Mogul' 43106 at Preston with the simple duty of keeping the sleeping cars warm; not an overtaxing assignment for the train crew. The sleeping cars were attached to the 2050 Barrow-Euston which departed from Preston at 2238, arriving in the capital at 0240. Sleeping car passengers were not ejected on to the streets of London at some unearthly hour as they were permitted to remain in their berths until 0730. 30 March 1968.

Left below: Preston Steam in the night (3): An unusual night view of 43106 at Preston with the engine facing north, and showing some of the steam age infrastructure and in particular the water crane and brazier; the latter was a simple device lit in the winter to provide warmth for the water supply. Once seen all over the system, they were also a welcome means of warming many hands, and a source of heat no doubt for countless cups of tea and bacon sandwiches! 30 March 1968.

Fleetwood Jameson Road Bridge (1): A brief excursion towards the Fylde. I have only two pictures of the Fleetwood Branch taken on the outskirts of the town. I seem to remember we were hanging around for ages here waiting for something of interest to come along, but the wait was worth it in the end as these are very rare pictures. '8F' 48715 is seen curving away from Fleetwood with a train, mostly of chemical wagons, heading in the Preston direction. Despite not being included in the infamous Beeching Report of 1963 for closure, that did not stop the line succumbing to passengers on 30 May (my birthday!) 1970. 4 June 1968.

Left above: Preston Derby Siding: Preston Station with a rather smart looking 'Black 5' 45444, heading the 3P24 0958 parcels to Barrow, standing at what was then Platform 5. Today since the re-signalling scheme of 1972 this is now Platform 3. In the foreground can be seen the buffer stops of the 'Derby Siding'. An oddity which remains to this day, but which was once the original alignment of the line into Platform 5, the origin of why it is named the 'Derby Siding' is unknown. 18 May 1968.

Left below: Preston Dock Street Sidings: 'Black 5' 44816 ambles in to Preston past Dock Street Sidings with an up freight in this undated October 1967 view. Behind can be seen part of the very impressive, former signal gantry for Maudlands Junction where the Blackpool line goes off to the left. Controlled from Preston numbers 4 and 5 Signal Boxes, this was the largest signal gantry in the country. Power signalling took over when the signal boxes closed on 5 February 1973 and this famous railway landmark was no more. 44816 has been signalled along the up main and will soon encounter its next signal for platforms 6 and 7. October 1967.

Blackpool South (2): Blackpool Illuminations railway style. A historic occasion as 'Black 5' 45212 has just arrived at Blackpool South with the penultimate service train on British Rail, and the last steam hauled train to have originated in London. I had the privilege of riding on this train. A Civic Reception awaited the 2048 from Preston and the portion off the 1705 from Euston. There were speeches and quite a crowd had gathered to witness the event. It was one of those special moments in time and the realisation had come to pass; no more would the steam hauled express ply its way along the tracks. 3 August 1968.

Left above: Fleetwood Jameson Road Bridge (2): I remember at the time complaining about the engine being tender first, but in retrospect it is a blessing in disguise as the going away shot of 48715 provides this superb panorama. To the right is Gala Gran Caravan Park. In the background the ICI Hillhouse Chemical Works (now demolished) dominate the skyline. Freight for the chemical works survived until 1999 and the line is now mothballed to this point pending preservation by the Poulton & Wyre Railway Society. 4 June 1968.

Left below: Blackpool South (1): I only managed a couple of decent pictures at Blackpool in steam days, both at Blackpool South and within a fortnight of each other. Here the enthusiasts look on 'Black 5' 45388 which has arrived with 1P58 2048 from Preston, a portion of the 1L79 1705 Euston-Carlisle. This Saturdays-only steam working would run for just the next two weeks as the clock ticked forward evermore to the end of steam. 20 July 1968.

Above: Garstang & Catterall: We are back on the West Coast Main Line heading north with a picture full of interest taken from a passing train, the 0907 Preston to Barrow to be precise, at Garstang & Catterall. 'Black 5' 45444 is standing on the dock road prior to crossing the bridge from the goods yard to the former branch platform, once the Garstang & Knott End Railway. One can almost imagine this as the 'Pilling Pig' freight train which ran until 1965 when the Light Railway finally closed. Garstang & Catterall Station closed on 3 February 1969. 15 June 1968.

Forton, Cleveley Bank Lane (1): Sunday track renewal has always been a feature of the West Coast main Line. On a Saturday, back in 1967, there was usually a special train of prefabricated track that ran as part of the CWR (Continuous Welded Rail) programme. This fairly rare combination of double headed '8Fs' 48687 + 48124 make for an impressive sight as they pound northward approaching Cleveley Bank Lane Bridge at Forton with a Fazakerley to Tebay rail train. These trains ran as Class 8 unfitted freight. 15 July 1967.

Left below: Forton: 'Black 5' 45013 approaching the Bay Horse down distant signal with the peak Saturdays only 24 June to 19 August 1M31 0910 Dundee to Blackpool North. The train is formed of all maroon, and mostly elderly ex LMR, coaching stock and if the front coach is anything to go by, plenty of enthusiasts enjoying another good run with steam. Departing from Carlisle at 1357 the train called only at Oxenholme (1507-1509) reaching Preston at 1551. Like almost all the Summer Saturday extras, the train did not convey any refreshment facilities; one can only muse over how many haggis sandwiches and scotch pies were consumed on the long journey south. 15 July 1967.

Bay Horse going north (1): The remains of the former down platform are very evident as 'Black 5' 44680 passes by on 1L27 1155 Euston to Carlisle with a portion for Windermere detached at Oxenholme. Note the green ex-Southern Region coaches in the formation, these had been displaced by the Bournemouth Line Electrification completed only the week before, and despatched north to replace pre-nationalisation stock. Repainting them into maroon would not be an option as the British Rail blue and grey livery for coaching stock was gradually taking over. 15 July 1967.

Left above: Forton, Cleveley Bank Lane (2): This location is about a couple of miles south of Bay Horse. Passing through pleasant open countryside is 'Black 5' 45435 with 1J80 1435 Barrow to Manchester Victoria. The up line had recently been re-laid as part of the CWR programme. Another feature of the steam era once so common and taken for granted were the line side telegraph poles, a particularly fine array of them on show in this picture. They have on many, and in particular main trunk lines, been replaced by modern cables being carried underground beside the track, one side effect is to make life easier for line side photographers! A nice display of White Elderflower and Great Hairy Willow Herb grace the left hand bank. 15 July 1967.

Left below: Bay Horse: Just about a mile from the present day Forton Service Station on the M6 motorway can be found the remains of Bay Horse Station. When the railway arrived here in 1840, the small cluster of houses formed a district known as Ellel. The station was named after the local pub conveniently situated yards from the tracks, thus the railway gave the present day village its name. The station was an early casualty, closing to passengers on 13 June 1960. There is still evidence of the former platforms, once connected by a subway, as 'Black 5' 44872 heads south with 3P89 empty coaching stock. I have been unable to trace the exact working as such trains often ran at short notice under 'Control Orders'. On the extreme left of the picture, my little blue Ford 100E mentioned in the introduction can be seen parked up in the former station yard; there were no security gates and palisade fences back then blocking access. 15 July 1967.

Bay Horse going north (2): 'Britannia' 70029 *Shooting Star* hurries past at 1705 with 1S80 1320 Euston to Glasgow Central and some blue and grey stock has found its way into the formation. This was another of those dated Summer Saturday trains running from 1 July to 2 September and surely one of the last chances to ride behind a 'Pacific' on an Anglo-Scottish express. Maybe the passengers (they are customers these days) could have done with a stop at Bay Horse for the pub as the train was not advertised as conveying refreshment facilities. The 'Britannia' would have come on the train at Crewe (departing at 1532) and, not stopping at Tebay for a banker over Shap, would run non-stop all the way to Carlisle arriving at 1823. 15 July 1967.

Oubeck: Leach House Lane (1): The fields at Leach House Lane, just to the south of Oubeck Loop, are bathed in evening sunshine as 'Black 5' 44822 heads south with 1J83 1810 Heysham to Manchester Victoria Boat Train. In the background a northbound freight can be spotted in the down loop at Oubeck. The Heysham-Belfast Ferry ran as a daily overnight sailing each way. The Saturday daytime sailings, and thus the corresponding boat trains, were confined to just six peak Saturdays of the season running throughout July and the first part of August. I had problems identifying them as they are in my notebook but not in the public timetable. It seems these workings were only agreed after the timetable had been published (a couple of months earlier than normal due to West Midland electrification) and therefore were only to be found in the supplement which I do not have. My special thanks to Ron Herbert for solving this mystery. The Heysham-Belfast passenger ferry ceased operation in April 1975 thus bringing to a conclusion the corresponding boat trains on the West Coast Main Line. 15 July 1967.

Approaching Hest Bank (1): The view looking south from the A5105 Marine Drive over-bridge built in 1933; a superb vantage point. Heading north is 'Black 5' 45435 approaching Hest Bank with 5L41 1405 Crewe Gretsy Lane to Carlisle Yard goods. It is sad to think all this traffic is now on the M6. Note the single line curving away in the background to the right towards Bare Lane, Morecambe and eventually Heysham. 19 July 1967.

Left above: Oubeck Leach House Lane (2): This train followed 44822 and its Manchester bound train by about ten minutes, so time to find a slightly different angle. Looking over the lush fields 'Black 5' 44917 is heading 1G41 1820 Heysham to Birmingham New Street with some elderly coaches of LMS origin included in the formation. Rather unusually this train was booked to run non-stop from Morecambe to Crewe. The nearest the West Coast Main Line gets to a Heysham Boat Train these days is the daily two-car sprinter running between Carnforth and Hest Bank, connecting Leeds to and from the Isle of Man Ferry. 15 July 1967.

Left below: Oubeck Leach House Lane (3): An ideal location for grabbing that extra shot, and I could not resist including the broadside view of 44917 heading south towards Birmingham with the engine set against a perfect blue evening sky; the coupling rods in the down position just adds to the impression of the power of steam. With the ex-LMS coach behind the tender the scene is indeed timeless. 15 July 1967.

Approaching Hest Bank (4): A low level view of the point where the single line from Hest Bank curves away towards Morecambe. Framed between the telegraph pole and the signal (the lower arm is the distant for Bare Lane) 'Britannia' 70014 *Iron Duke* heads north with a lengthy unidentified freight. I do recall after a superb evening's photography here adjourning to the fish and chip shop by the nearby station; they really tasted good that night! 19 July 1967.

Left above: Approaching Hest Bank (2): Block trains were a fairly novel feature in the late 1960s, and certainly one of the few to be steam hauled was 7L00 1115 Oakleigh Sidings (Northwich) to Whitehaven Corkickle No. 1. The train, known to the railway enthusiast as 'The Soda Ash,' is seen heading north with '8F' 48631 heading a rake of the very distinctive and smart looking 'Covhop' wagons. 19 July 1967.

Left below: Approaching Hest Bank (3): One of the joys of railway photography is the joy of the unexpected bonus. Spending a glorious Wednesday evening on the A5105 Marine Drive over-bridge in glorious light, the appearance of 'Black 5' 45221 heading north on the weed killing train was a complete surprise; I was not expecting that one, but am not complaining. One simply went out and stood by the line-side and took what was on offer as there were no mobile phones, gen lines or websites back in 1967; more fun I think. 19 July 1967.

Morecambe West End: A view from West End Road Bridge at Morecambe. On the left, 'Black 5' 44948 is leaving tender first for the former LNWR line to Bare Lane with 9T50 1230 Heysham to Carnforth trip working, and is about to pass 45373 on its Heysham-bound train previously seen at Bare Lane. The line in the middle is the once electrified, and now closed, former Midland Railway route to Lancaster Green Ayre, and the line on the far right goes to Heysham. Thus all trains going to Heysham now have to reverse at Morecambe. Note the former Euston Road Station in the background, now a builder's yard. 21 July 1967.

Left above: Bare Lane (1): Time now to take a trip down the line to Morecambe and Heysham and we call in at Bare Lane. The station then was well kept and the roses are growing well; it says a lot about the neat and tidy railway scene of forty-seven years ago. 'Black 5' 44971 passes by with an unidentified empty stock working from Morecambe towards Lancaster and the South. As mentioned when discussing Bay Horse these trains often ran at short notice due to traffic requirements and this was another bonus picture. The station is still open; the signal box not closing until 9 December 2012. 21 July 1967.

Left below: Bare Lane (2): Looking the other way at Bare Lane towards Hest Bank and Lancaster, 'Black 5' 45373 has charge of 7P11 1050 Ribble Sidings (Preston) to Heysham Harbour goods. We shall follow this train all the way to its destination. Note the brake van marshalled next to the engine as it was mandatory to have one at each end of the train on this line due to the reversal at Morecambe to reach Heysham. The station is still open and other than the nuclear flask train for Heysham Power Station, little freight now passes through here. 21 July 1967.

Heysham: We sign off our visit to Heysham with a look at 'Black 5' 44983 basking in the evening sun with Money Lane Bridge behind. The engine had worked in on 3M00 from Leeds as we shall see in the next picture, and is seen prior to turning to return with the 1946 Heysham Harbour to Stourton (Leeds) freight. 19 July 1967.

Left above: Heysham Money Close Lane: 'Black 5' 45373 has reversed and been turned on the turntable at Morecambe and is now approaching Heysham Harbour. Seen from the delightfully named Money Close Lane over-bridge the train is running in under the former catenary masts, evidence of the electrification for trains on the former Midland Railway route from Lancaster Green Ayre abandoned on New Year's Day 1966. Also note next to the front brake van are a couple of 'Oxfit' cattle wagons, once another common sight on our railways. 21 July 1967.

Left below: Heysham Harbour: Looking the other way from Money Lane Bridge, it is hard to realise Heysham Harbour ever looked like this. 'Black 5' 45373 is arriving with its 7P11 freight from Ribble Sidings, Preston. The yard pilot Class 08 diesel shunter D3566 is actively engaged for there is much traffic in the Harbour Sidings to keep it busy. Today Heysham is a Container Port and just two lines of rail survive, one to serve the daily passenger train connecting with the Isle of Man Ferry, the other to serve the nuclear power station. Everything else has been swept away or given over to the lorry. Note the former Midland Railway Signal Box. 21 July 1967.

Hest Bank: Back to Hest Bank, the only place where the West Coast Main Line actually meets the sea, and the view looking north from the A5105 Marine Drive over-bridge. Top left of the picture a glimpse of the wide expanse of Morecambe Bay. To the top right behind Cinderella Footbridge, named after a nearby Children's Home, is the former Hest Bank Station (closed 3 February 1969.) Not in the best looking condition 'Black 5' 44983 heads for Bare Lane with 3M00 1348 Leeds City to Heysham Harbour parcels, yes the railway did actually once run trains like that. Of particular interest is the leading vehicle behind the engine, a smart Southern Region PMV (Parcels Miscellaneous Van) far away from its home territory. When these vans eventually returned to the Southern Region they passed through the carriage wash at Eastleigh or Clapham Junction keeping them in excellent external condition. PMVs also had a guard's periscope window on the roof and one can be spotted on this van. 19 July 1967.

Pasture Lane Bridge: From its brief encounter with the sea at Hest Bank, the West Coast Main Line turns inland again. Not far from Morecambe Lodge is Pasture Lane Bridge where we see 'Black 5' 45374 heading south with a well loaded ballast train, again one of those unexpected workings which just came along at the right time. The small township of Bolton-le-Sands which we shall shortly visit is in the background. 19 July 1967.

Bolton-le-Sands (2): The station lay just to the south of Carnforth in a mostly rural setting and was a delightful little place. It closed to all traffic as from 3 February 1969 and no trace remains today. Shortly after the passage of 92058, 'Black 5' 45054 displaying Class 'K' head lamps (mineral or stopping goods) heads south on a lovely summer afternoon with the local freight trip 9T50 1415 Carnforth to Heysham Moss. 19 July 1967.

Left above: Pasture Lane: I took an afternoon walk in the country; what better than a stroll down Pasture Lane under the trees as '8F' 48696 runs alongside northbound heading for Carnforth Shed, more than likely light engine from Heysham. The view here is recognisable today but with growth, the railway now electrified and with a higher and more substantial fence, photography now is difficult. This is what a summer afternoon's amble by the railway should be like. 19 July 1967.

Left below: Bolton-le-Sands (1): The view looking north from the station footbridge. Note the low height of the platforms; clearly visible on the down platform is the little set of portable steps, thoughtfully provided to assist passengers boarding and alighting from trains. One can only wonder in this day and age of Health and Safety how many pages the Safety Case would have been, and what about the risk assessment? The mind boggles. '9F' 92058 is seen heading south with the 8F96 1001 Carlisle to Birkenhead freight. 19 July 1967.

Above: Carnforth No. 1 Signal Box (1): An unexpected pass at Carnforth No.1, when the photographers were waiting patiently for 'Black 5' 45054 to depart for the south with its freight train. Without warning 'Britannia' 70013 *Oliver Cromwell* appeared on a northbound express, 1S71 1327 Fridays only Manchester Victoria/Liverpool Exchange—Glasgow/Edinburgh, a train normally diesel hauled then; we were not expecting steam on that one. Not quite the planned shot but very acceptable. 21 July 1967.

Below: Carnforth No. 1 Signal Box (2): An overall view of the south end of Carnforth with some splendid track work on view. The coaling tower of the locomotive shed can be seen in the left background with a plume of steam rising. Seen from Crag Bank Bridge '9F' 92166 partly obscures the view of Carnforth No 1 Signal Box as she heads south with the lengthy 8F96 1001 Carlisle to Birkenhead freight. 21 July 1967.

Carnforth No. 1 (3): The going away shot from Crag Bank Bridge at Carnforth of 92166
heading south, and a splendid rear-end view of the imposing gantry which was the Carnforth
No 1 down home signal. From right to left the signals read: shed entrance signal via the
'Dessert' road; down loop; Furness Line with calling on arm; and down main line with lower
distant arm for Carnforth No. 2. Both signal boxes were closed and the signals replaced with
colour lights when this area of Carnforth was placed under the control of Preston Power Signal
Box on 22 January 1973. 21 July 1967.

Carnforth Grosvenor Road footbridge: A striking view of activity at Carnforth. 'Black 5' 45025 is seen with a ballast train. In the background far right can be seen the passenger station, next to the left a rather busy looking Furness Yard, further left again the locomotive shed with its coaling stage prominent. In front of the latter note the Wagon Repair Shops still in use today by West Coast Railways. The sidings on the far left are the shed outlet to the main line, known locally as 'The Dessert.' 45025 has been preserved on the Strathspey Railway. Grosvenor Road footbridge was demolished in the early 1970s when the line was electrified. 25 July 1968.

Carnforth Shed (2): The second view from Hunting Hill. 45234 has been turned, behind is '8F' 48519 coming on shed. Locomotives were turned by crews on shed turning duties who coaled, watered, turned and put the locomotives away in the order they were required for other duties. Above the arm of the red steam crane is the warehouse, which at one time had its own shunting engine. Across the tracks is the Railway Club; one wonders just how many pints were consumed in there after a hard day's work on steam. Top left is Carnforth East Junction Signal Box, it is amazing just how many signals one can spot in the picture. 14 July 1967.

Left below: Carnforth Shed (1): The view from Hunting Hill in the evening sunshine. The public footpath was a marvellous vantage point to watch the activity on the Shed. 'Black 5' 45234 is being turned with driver Tommy Owen (one who knew how to 'thrash 'em') and his unknown fireman in charge of the operation. On the right are some stored engines including 48425 and 46400, with the green ex-London, Tilbury & Southend tank *Thundersley*. To the left, the *Hornby Dublo* red steam crane, the pride of the Carnforth fitters and the wooden shed, used by the Signal and Telegraph Department. Behind is the still open Carnforth Station Junction Box, where the lines for the 'Furness and Midland Joint' and the 'Furness' divided; the still extant but out of use footbridge; and a nice view of the town itself. 14 July 1967.

Carnforth Shed (3): The final view from Hunting Hill with '8F' 48519 under the 1944 built coaling stage (where for many years Charlie Coates was the man in charge) and 'Black 5' 44886 behind. A Government grant in 1942 enabled Carnforth Shed to be rebuilt and extended to provide better facilities for the war effort and was thus a very modern shed; one reason why it lasted until the end of steam. 14 July 1967.

Right above: Carnforth Shed, The old and the new (1): Steam and rare diesels. 'Black 5' 44877 is outnumbered by the growing number of diesels now using the shed. To the left is Class 17 'Clayton' D8506, a member of one of probably the most unsuccessful diesel classes constructed. Built 1962-65, withdrawal started the month this picture was taken and all had gone by December 1971. Behind stands a gleaming brand new Class 50 D419, just two months old. This engine would fare much better until it was withdrawn as 50 019 in September 1990. 18 May 1968.

Right below: Carnforth Shed, The old and the new (2): Proof indeed that the two types of motive power shared the same facilities alongside each other. Peering out of Carnforth shed are left 'Black 5' 44874, and right Class 28 D5705, one of the 20 Metropolitan-Vickers built machines with Co-Bo wheel arrangement (six-wheel bogie one end, four-wheel the other), unique on British Rail and rarely photographed. This is one picture where the diesel is probably more interesting than the steam! Built 1958-59, they were unsuccessful and had all been with withdrawn by September 1969. 18 May 1968.

Carnforth Old Iron Works Bridge: Looking west out towards the Cumbrian Coast with Morecambe Bay in the background, the view from the former Old Iron Works Bridge. It is still there, but in the past it used to carry the steelworks line from the shore to the slag heaps. 'Black 5' 44809 approaches Carnforth with an early morning freight from Barrow, crewed by Carnforth men who were in the Furness link (nicknamed 'The Old Man's Link.') This locomotive was a favourite with the crews and fitters at Carnforth Shed since it had been allocated there for most of its working life. 20 July 1968.

Left above: Carnforth Shed: Carnforth Shed was rebuilt in 1944 and survives today as the depot for the West Coast Railway Company. I could not resist a last look with, as far as I know, the only 'Pacific' ever allocated to the Shed: 70013 *Oliver Cromwell*. The engine was based there primarily to work the farewell steam rail tours; many well documented in this publication. I think the Parliamentarian would have been proud that his engine had outlasted all the Royalty of the steam era: the 'Kings'; 'Castles'; 'Duchesses'; and the 'Princess Royals' to name just a few. He carried the banner to the very end. 18 May 1968.

Left below: Carnforth Bottom End Yard: We now move on to Cumbrian Coast line for a trip out to Barrow. 'Black 5' 44894 with 3P24 0958 Preston to Barrow vans, one of the last regularly hauled steam trains and just about the last time it was steam hauled, caught on camera passing the rarely photographed Carnforth Bottom End Yard which was quite extensive, and in this view not exactly bursting with traffic. The load for the 44894 does not look particularly heavy. 20 July 1968.

Carnforth Old Iron Works Bridge: Looking the other way from the Old Iron Works Bridge, the view looking east with Carnforth Bottom End Yard just beyond Sand Lane road bridge. I could not resist including the going away shot of 44809. With the signpost to the far right, the green fields, an attractive little road over-bridge, and a nice house in the country to the left, a picture that sums up rural England, when the steam engine just went about its daily business as part of the everyday scene and nobody really took much notice of it, then all of a sudden it was gone. 20 July 1968.

Silverdale: There is a saying that every picture tells a story, well this one tells more than most. The penultimate day of steam working on service trains was Saturday 3 August 1968, a day that started rather dull and wet. The sun has just come out for this historic view of 'Black 5' 45231 at Silverdale on its last working before entering preservation, a ballast train from Waterslack Quarry to Farington Junction. This turned out to be the next to last steam hauled ballast train on British Rail, the last steam hauled train on the Cumbrian Coast Line, and the last steam hauled revenue earning working on the West Coast Main Line to run the full length from Lancaster to Preston. From information later obtained from the Power Controller's Sheets in the Divisional Freight Movements Office at Preston, the following day a Class 5 is reported to have worked a ballast from Carnforth to Oubeck (near to where I photographed the Heysham Boat Trains). The number was not recorded and no photographic evidence exists since everyone was elsewhere in the North West chasing all the rail tours, so it was not observed either, thus the above working was not quite the last in all the aspects originally thought but it meets most of the criteria. Railway history is never easy! 3 August 1968.

Ulverston: The Saturday 0958 Preston to Barrow Parcels was an unbalanced working; at Barrow the locomotive was turned and watered and then returned to Lostock Hall Shed light engine, which does seem a bit of a waste of resources. On such a move we catch up with 'Black 5' 45353 passing through Ulverston Station, the jewel of the crown in the Furness Railway. The imposing canopies and the clock tower of 1873 vintage have fairly recently been restored. The unusual platform layout was designed for easy access by passengers from the south to change for the onetime branch to Lakeside, which closed to passengers 6 September 1965 and to all traffic two years later. The top three and a half miles of this line have re-opened as the preserved Lakeside & Haverthwaite Railway. 15 June 1968.

Left above: Arnside Knott: Late on a Saturday morning towards the end of steam, the magnificent view from Arnside Knott, 522 feet above sea level (and I have no idea what that is metres, nor do I wish to know). An unidentified 'Black 5' working 3P24 0958 Preston to Barrow parcels crosses the River Kent, here the boundary of the National Park, on Arnside Viaduct and the tide is in. The Lake District forming one of the most scenic backdrops a photographer could ever wish for; I certainly chose the right day for this one. 8 June 1968.

Left below: Grange-Over-Sands: On a beautiful summer's morning by the shore of Morecambe Bay 'Black 5' 44911 pulls away from Grange-Over-Sands along the sea wall with 1P39 0835 Barrow to London Euston, a portion that will be attached at Lancaster Castle to 1A40 0820 Carlisle to Euston and would reach the capital at 1400. The six coach formation is a nice mosaic of blue and grey, then maroon all following in repeat order. 20 July 1967.

Bentham: High summer at High Bentham. We catch up again with 70013 working the 'Dalesman No. 2' rail tour previously seen at Lydgate and the climb to Copy Pit. We did a lot of miles that day in the little 100E. The cattle graze on and pay little attention in the summer heat as the special train passes the former loops on the approach to Bentham Station from the Carnforth direction. The station is still open, the loops long since removed. 16 June 1968.

Left above: Barrow-In-Furness Station: Barrow Station was formerly known as Barrow Central. The present day station was built as part of the 1955 announced Modernisation Programme and was opened in 1959; a replacement for the station destroyed in the Second World War by enemy bombing. Abbey Road Bridge provides a good view of the rather spacious and neat and tidy looking station with 'Black 5' 45353 arriving with the 3P24 0958 Parcels from Preston. The return light engine working was photographed as seen on page 75. 15 June 1968.

Left below: Melling: The other line that links in at Carnforth with the West Coast is the 'Little' North Western, so we have in effect turned right and are now heading east again. On the joint former Midland and Furness Companies section 'Black 5' 44874 is seen passing through the former Melling Station (closed 5 May 1952) and is approaching Melling Tunnel with 1T80, a British Rail 'Last Days of Steam' rail tour, on its return to Preston and Manchester via Hellifield and Blackburn. This engine was a late replacement for 70013 which had failed on the outward leg of the tour; steam engines did fail now and again, they were not infallible. 2 June 1968.

Giggleswick (1): A period of activity at the normally quiet wayside station of Giggleswick as 'Black 5' 44877 has arrived with 9T50 1305 Carnforth to Skipton pick up goods train, and shunting is now in progress. The train has been split and the fireman is climbing back on board the engine. The ground disc signal indicates that the road is set for access to the sidings on the right. Plenty of interest in this view looking west; note the rather sturdy water tower on the left. 19 July 1968.

Left above: Clapham (1): There was another Clapham Junction hidden away in the West Riding of Yorkshire. The course of the recently demolished line to Ingleton can be seen going straight on, the line to Carnforth curves away to the left by the signal box. The station remains open, but today lacks the charm of its 1960s appearance. A thought: if one were to spend a couple of days at the more famous Clapham Junction in South West London, one would probably see more trains there in that period than would be seen here in a year. 16 June 1968.

Left below: Clapham (2): On a hot Sunday afternoon with the Pennine Foothills barely visible in the haze 70013 heads away from 'the other' Clapham Junction for Skipton with the 'Dalesman No. 2' rail tour. Behind the train the viaduct and the station can be seen. The number of cars parked on this normally quiet road indicates this was a popular location, and I seem to remember the dry stone wall most of the photographers were standing on had difficulty coping with the numbers using the facility; I don't think much damage was done that day. 16 June 1968.

Giggleswick (4): Some former Midland Railway Company infrastructure still in use at Giggleswick station in 1968. The typical station name board, a not particularly tall oil lamp and the neat and tidy platform with its little garden provide a rather welcoming scene. Behind a generous supply of mineral wagons can be seen in the former Private Siding of P. W. Spencer, now eradicated under the Giggleswick bypass. The eagle-eyed will spot the red wagon to the right of the lamppost is stencilled 'House Coal Concentration,' obviously here in use for stone traffic from Giggleswick. One assumes another Control Office arrangement. 19 July 1968.

Left above: Giggleswick (2): A typical Midland Railway signal box to the left and to the right 44877 is pushing its train in to the Private Siding which served the limestone works of P. W. Spencer. What a charming scene. The local pick up goods had been an integral part of the railway ever since there had been railways, serving stations big and small with all manner of traffic. The economics of working such traffic had been called in to question by Doctor Beeching in his report four years previous and the days of such trains were numbered. 19 July 1968.

Left below: Giggleswick (3): An almost branch line view as the driver of 44877 is seen concentrating as he pushes his train into the Private Siding to pick up mineral wagons. A once common everyday scene, yet by the time the film came back from the processing lab, it was all history as the steam age had run its course. The limestone traffic here ceased in the early 1970s when the siding closed and virtually no trace remains today. Now there are very few private sidings and the pick-up goods are long since a memory. 19 July 1968.

Hellifield (1): Both a country junction and a railway town, Hellifield was once a hive of activity but the station is looking a bit the worse for wear in this view taken looking east from the down platform as the steam age nears its end. The former bay platform for Carlisle trains will see no more use. There is a look of dereliction and the weeds are starting to take over, it was sad to see stations like this being allowed to deteriorate. Here the story has a happy ending. Although still open but unstaffed since the mid 1970s, the buildings were restored and returned to commercial use in the late 1980s and the train service has been improved in recent years, making Hellifield an ideal starting point for a trip over the scenic Settle & Carlisle line. The station is well worth a visit today. 1 June 1968.

Left above: Settle Junction (1): In my experience of the North West, steam and diesel combinations were not that common. Approaching Settle Junction, Class 25 D7624 and 'Black 5' 45206 are the motive power for 4N28 1212 Heysham Moss to Leeds Neville Hill oil tanks, this train at the time booked for such traction. The diesel is showing the incorrect head code, the driver has got that one wrong! The Settle & Carlisle line, on one of the few occasions I saw it in sunshine, can be seen running in to the right. 19 July 1968.

Left below: Settle Junction (2): Shunting at Giggleswick has been completed and mineral wagons attached as 44877 with 9T50 1305 Carnforth to Skipton pick-up goods joins the still open former Midland Railway route to Scotland at Settle Junction. The previous picture of the oil train was taken from the bridge behind the train where one can pick out the start of 'The Long Drag,' but that is another story. The scene here today is almost unchanged. 19 July 1968.

Gisburn Tunnel: After emerging from the 157-yard Gisburn Tunnel on the penultimate weekend of steam 'Black 5' 45156 is seen passing a fine display of summer flowers (with Rosebay Willowherb prominent) heading for Hellifield on the line from Blackburn with 1T80, a G. C. Enterprises special from Stockport to Carnforth and back. The tunnel with its ornamental stone portals was built at the insistence of Lord Ribblesdale who demanded that the railway passed through the grounds of Gisburne Park underground so as not to spoil the view. 4 August 1968.

Left above: Hellifield (2): A rather pastoral view taken from the station platform as 70013 stands on the access line to the turntable at Hellifield and a crew change takes place. The engine had been detached from the British Rail Scottish Region Grand Tour No. 5, which we encountered at Blackrod, and D1773 has taken over for the return to Bonnie Scotland. Surely this will be one of the last steam engines to use the basic facilities that still remained at Hellifield. Note behind the tender the water softening plant installed by the LMS. 1 June 1968.

Left below: Hellifield Turntable: Rather surprisingly the 60-foot turntable installed at Hellifield in 1940 survived along with the watering facilities after the locomotive shed had closed in June 1963. I seem to recall there was some concern whether the 'Britannia' Pacific would actually fit, but all was well and the operation to turn the locomotive is seen under way. Once facing in the right direction the engine ran light to Lostock Hall Shed for further rail tour duty the following day. To the right is Hellifield Station, with the still open Hellifield South Junction Signal Box in the background. 1 June 1968.

Yealand: We are now back on the West Coast Main Line at Yealand, just to the Carnforth side of Burton & Holme, heading north for 'them there hills.' Heading in the up direction is 'Britannia' 70015 *Apollo* with the rather lengthy, morning, fitted freight from Carlisle to Crewe. The northern fells start to loom in the far distance. 19 July 1967.

Left above: Leeds City (1): Steam North East. It is just over 36 miles from Hellifield to Leeds which is geographically beyond the scope of this book, but the train is certainly not as this is a North West based working, and a historic occasion as well. 'Black 5' 45310 stands at Leeds City with the 0332 to Halifax, and (as far as I know) the very last steam working out of Leeds. As we pulled out I noticed there were not many people about to witness the occasion, but that is hardly surprising bearing in mind the hour! 18 May 1968.

Left below: Leeds City (2): The view at Leeds City looking west into the night as 45310 waits to steam in to history. At Halifax the train was combined with the 0210 York-Manchester which 45310 worked forward departing at 0438. It was also the last scheduled steam working in the Manchester area to display class 'A' (express) headlamps. The locomotive then was stabled at Newton Heath Shed where, as previously seen, I photographed it at a more reasonable hour the following day. 18 May 1968.

Oxenholme: 70011 heading south and signalled into the up loop at Oxenholme. To the left is the branch platform for Windermere, on the far left the exit line from the former locomotive shed, to the right by Oxenholme No. 2 Signal Box an Engineer's mess van is parked in one of the goods docks with the rather charming little goods office behind. Note the 1960s scene completed by the 'Lyons Maid' van delivering the ice cream. 20 July 1967.

Left above: Milnthorpe: We were stuck in the queue for the traffic lights at Milnthorpe, a notorious bottleneck on the old A6 in pre-M6 days, when smoke was detected in the distance. With apologies to the motorists behind us, the car was abandoned and a dash made to the bridge for the unexpected appearance of 'Jubilee' 45697 *Achilles* on the southbound vans. It was well worth the angry looks and toots at the time. The 'Jubilees' were a rare sight on the West Coast line by this time. 19 July 1967.

Left below: Hincaster: As we head further north in to what was once Westmorland and since 1974 now part of Cumbria, the background is just starting to show more signs of the forthcoming hill country. Just to the Carlisle side of the former Hincaster Junction a light '9F' heads south through the pastoral countryside; its motion glistening in the evening sunshine. 18 July 1967.

Tebay Shed (2): The Ghost of Christmas past. My final visit to Tebay Shed was on a December evening just before Christmas in December 1967, a couple of weeks before the shed closed. The former LNWR shed was rebuilt 1948-50 with four roads, shown to good effect in this long time exposure in the still, cold, December night air. You the reader have an invitation to study the picture and absorb the unique atmosphere of this lonely railway outpost as the 'Standard 4s' take their night rest. 13 December 1967.

Left above: Tebay: At the Carlisle end of the Lune Gorge is Tebay, seen here looking north before the arrival of the M6 Motorway. This is a complete panorama of an isolated railway community. Beyond the River Lune, the former Exchange Sidings are packed with goods wagons, the roof of the former Tebay No. 1 Signal Box can be spotted with the railway built terraces behind. A plume of steam rises from Tebay Shed, our next port of call. It is a very different scene today. Tebay or not Tebay, oh for a summer's evening. 22 July 1967.

Left below: Tebay Shed (1): In the autumn afternoon sunshine a couple of 'Standard 4's' stand in steam outside Tebay Shed, with the hills behind. Nearest the camera 75037 is standing with 75024 alongside, both looking a bit the worse for wear. The primary function of the depot at this time was to provide engines for banking assistance over both Grayrigg and Shap inclines and local freight trip working, but time was fast running out for this lonely outpost of steam and such duties. October 1967.

Tebay Shed (5): Forget not the smell of hissing steam and piston valve, exemplified by 75030 at rest outside Tebay Shed on that memorable December night. It was a lengthy time exposure to obtain this truly atmospheric picture, ably assisted by the shed foreman who provided a portable brazier to keep the two photographers warm, complete with mug of tea. The hospitality of the 'Men of Steam' was second to none, it was a wonderful experience to visit Tebay Shed in the darkness of the bleak mid-winter. 13 December 1967.

Left above: Tebay Shed (3): A locomotive we shall be seeing quite a lot of in the pages to come on its Shap banking duties, 75026 has been coaled and watered and stands inside Tebay Shed awaiting its next call of duty. This is what the interior of a working steam shed was like at night, the not too bright lights mingle with the haze of soot and steam in a unique atmosphere where there is coal, oil, dust and the sound of hissing steam. To many I think the nearest thing to Heaven on Earth. 13 December 1967.

Left below: Tebay Shed (4): 75039 peers out from Tebay Shed in to the December night but she is cold and will not steam again. Careful examination of the tender reveals it bears the chalked legend 'COND' in other words already withdrawn from service. This engine will have only one more journey to make, and that will be to a scrapyard in Scotland. The finale for 75039 had come at the end of September 1967 after a working life of only 14 years and one month. 13 December 1967.

Birkbeck Viadict: At 1940 on a fine summer's evening 'Black 5' 44761 is seen in the beautiful Westmorland scenery climbing away from Birkbeck Viaduct with 1P28 1428 Crewe to Carlisle parcels running about 40 minutes early. It was not unusual for such a train to have a Class 1 head code, the 1A65 1835 Kendal to Euston parcels Mondays to Fridays was another such example. 22 July 1967.

Left above: Tebay Shed (6): A final view of steam in the night at Tebay shed with a broadside picture of 75030 simmering away in the yard. The lighting was not exactly bright and this needed a two-minute time exposure to bring the scene to life. That brazier and mug of tea were most welcome! 13 December 1967.

Left below: Tebay North Eastern Yard: Tebay was also once a junction with the former LNER Stainmore line which closed in January 1962, although a short stretch at the Tebay end lasted until the end of 1963. In the former LNER goods yard which was retained in use at this time, primarily as a depot for the Long Welded Rail Programme, we see '8F' 48046 and a rather busy scene. The rather low platform to the left will not see another passenger. Today this side of the station has been completely obliterated. Further left we see the former Tebay No 2 Signal Box situated at the foot of the incline over Shap, the next stage of our journey north. 20 July 1967.

Scout Green (1): Between Greenholme and Shap Wells the railway met a minor road at a level crossing. To generations of railway photographers and devotees of steam this was an iconic place, the classic setting of Scout Green. In the land of dry stone walls '9F' 92224 slogs up the hill past the isolated signal box with 5L41 1405 Crewe Gresty Lane to Carlisle Yard with 75026 providing banking assistance. 20 July 1967.

Left above: This train was of some considerable length with as varied a mixture of parcels and goods vans one would ever see. 'Standard 4' 75026 is hard at work banking the train to Shap Summit, and provides the view of Birkbeck Viaduct; a three arch span of brick and stone taking the railway approx. 45 feet over the little stream. 22 July 1967.

Left below: A third view from the taken from the same spot as the train climbs towards Greenholme. A magnificent panorama of steam in the landscape and hardly a cloud in the sky. I will leave the reader to imagine the sound on a still June evening. Here the train is at the point where the 1 in 146 grade from Lune Bridge near Tebay steepens to the 1 in 75 climb all the way to Shap Summit. 22 July 1967.

Scout Green (4): It is not often the railway photographer has the chance to take four classic pictures of one train in full glorious early evening sunshine on Shap, so I make no apologies for this final view of 92224 and 75026 heading away north from Scout Green. High upon the lonely Fells the railway here is at one with nature; the grazing sheep are blissfully unaware of the drama before their very eyes. A scene that reminds us of how the railway here taxed the Men of Steam to their very limits at times; this is how Shap was conquered. 20 July 1967.

Left above: Scout Green (2): A not too common view as most photographers pointed their cameras in the other direction here so the 'going away' shot of 92224 merits inclusion as not only showing the scene looking north at Scout Green, but also just how finely the line over Shap Fell (opened 15 December 1846) was engineered by Joseph Locke. Locke insisted that severe gradients were a perfectly acceptable feature of railway working, and indeed this gave the Lancaster & Carlisle an atmosphere of its own and problems for the Operating Department not finally overcome until the advent of the modern day diesels and electrics. 20 July 1967.

Left below: Scout Green (3): The view of the banker 'Standard 4' 75026 is worthy of inclusion in its own right. The train crew appear to be taking a slight breather even though the engine is working hard to assist 92224 up the 1 in 75 gradient. This is Scout Green at its very best. The level crossing (abolished in the early 1970s when the line was electrified) and signal box (closed 16 April 1973) both show up well behind the train with the Howgill Hills in the distance. 20 July 1967.

Shap Wells (1): The classic scene at Shap Wells. In the evening sunshine '9F' 92208 banked by 'Standard 4' 75026 make a fine sight as they pound up the 1 in 75 incline with 5L41 1405 Crewe Gresty Lane to Carlisle Yard Goods, booked to pass Shap Summit at 1813. Of particular interest in this ordinary, everyday, general merchandise freight train are the yellow continental wagons which, in those long ago days before the Channel Tunnel, reached our shores by train ferry. 22 July 1967.

Left above: Scout Green (5): Geographically these two pictures are slightly out of order as they are immediately to the south of the former Scout Green Signal Box. Viewed in the moorland setting from the minor road at Scout Green 'Black 5' 45133 has not called in at Tebay for a banker and is working hard up the hill with 3L14 1328 Crewe to Carlisle and a lengthy mixture of goods and parcel vans. 20 July 1967.

Left below: Scout Green (6): The wide open spaces here gave plenty of opportunity for photography and thus the chance to try out something different, hence a second look at 45133 and a broad side view with the engine running parallel to a dry stone wall. The driver seems to be enjoying a look at the passing scenery. I suspect the fireman is working hard as the engine is unassisted with a heavy load on the 1 in 75 to the summit. 20 July 1967.

Shap Wells (4): A few yards further north from the above view of 70039 which was taken from the ridge in the right background, 'Black 5' 44876 is seen working hard up the hill with its load of six coaches, well within the capabilities of the class, putting out a fine display of black smoke with 1L27 1155 Euston-Carlisle. A portion for Windermere would have been detached at Oxenholme. Judging by the number of heads out of the window in the first coach the railway enthusiasts are enjoying the last summer of steam over Shap; departing Oxenholme at 1627 the train was allowed 47 minutes for the 32 and a quarter miles to Penrith. What a pleasant way to spend a Saturday afternoon. 22 July 1967.

Left above: Shap Wells (2): The duty banker in the period of time I was in the area was 75026 and is working hard to assist 922208 up the hill, providing a fine display of black smoke which is blowing well over the fells. 75026 was an old friend, being a former Western Region engine based in my home town locomotive shed of Laira, Plymouth 83D, for the first two years of its life from May 1954. She was withdrawn when Tebay shed closed on 31 December 1967. I wonder how many men gazing at the brand new 75026 in Plymouth in 1954 would have imagined she would not manage 14 years of service. 22 July 1967.

Left below: Shap Wells (3): 'Britannia' 70039 Sir Christopher Wren is going well up the grade unassisted on a nice rake of maroon coaches with 1S80 1320 Euston-Glasgow Central, which had by now become the last 'Pacific' hauled Anglo-Scottish Express. One can still sample the same view today but it has changed, not for the better, with the railway being electrified in the early 1970s and the M6 motorway now dominating the isolated ridge behind the train. Shap as it was. 22 July 1967.

Shap Fell (1): One of my favourite photographs of all time. The sun has just come out and it stayed out for the rest of the day. 'Black 5' 44920 working 3L09 1018 Crewe to Carlisle Parcels is about to enter Shap Cutting on the last lap towards the summit which it is due to pass at 1322. To me this picture portrays the sheer beauty of Shap and what a location to see steam hard at work. Those of us who were able to tread the paths and green fields of Shap in search of steam were indeed privileged. Today one would find a forest planted where I am standing, the railway electrified and the M6 motorway for a background. 22 July 1967.

Right above: Shap Wells (2): A view from the east side of the line looking west. 'Black 5' 45455 looks very much at home in the dramatic landscape with Shap Fell as a backdrop. The train is climbing away from Shap Wells towards the summit. We were a bit 'wrong footed' for this and was not expecting steam, hence the photographers are on the shadow side of the train, yet I feel in a way that adds a little to the scene as both the landscape and the magnificent dry stone wall show up well. 22 July 1967.

Right below: Shap Wells (3): 'Standard 4' 75026 is in fine fettle and leaving a nice trail of smoke as it gives 45455 a helping hand up the hill with 1S54 1045 Blackpool North to Dundee. This was another high season Saturday only train running 24 June to 19 August and booked to pass Shap Summit at 1255. I suspect some of the passengers are having a smoke as the drama unfolds in the fells. How it can be a criminal offence nowadays for someone like myself to enjoy a puff of the pipe whilst viewing scenery like this from the carriage window is beyond me. 22 July 1967.

Shap Cutting (1): Racing southbound down the hill from Shap summit 'Black 5' 45072 emerges from the summit cutting in glorious evening sunshine with 1M32 1326 Glasgow Central to Morecambe Promenade, another high season Saturdays only train which ran 1 July to 19 August. This train gave an opportunity for a good non-stop journey with steam. It was booked to depart from Carlisle at 1612 then run non-stop to Carnforth arriving at 1747, a distance of just under 63 miles. The view of 44920 working the 3L09 parcels up the hill at lunchtime was taken from the mound to the top left of the picture. 22 July 1967.

Left above: Shap Fell (4): The wide open spaces of Shap provided adequate opportunities for photography of steam in the landscape and capturing the aura of the moorland setting, shown to good effect with this view of 45455 and 75026 heading towards the summit cutting with the Blackpool-Dundee, the leading engine more or less in the same place as we saw 44920 working 3L09 parcels. One could probably get a similar view today from the hard shoulder of the M6 motorway, but I feel not quite so dramatic. 22 July 1967.

Left below: Shap Fell (5): A third variation of the view of a train approaching the summit cutting, this time a far more distant view of an unknown 'Black 5' on a down goods. Across the fields cattle graze by a lonely farm, and the delivery van is making its morning calls along the country lane; is this not rural England at its best? The poet Wordsworth objected to the building of the railway over Shap Fell; would he have not relished steam in such a setting? The view today has been spoilt by the M6 motorway; now what would Wordsworth have had to say about that? 21 July 1967.

Shap Station (1): The Lancaster & Carlisle Railway built a nice little station to serve the village of Shap, seen here looking south as 'Black 5' 44911 passes through on 5L01 0655 Crewe Gresty Lane to Carlisle Goods. Closed to all traffic as from 1 July 1968 the main building to the right survives in use as a house, but the rather ornate canopy is a memory, as is the charming little waiting shelter on the up platform to the left. Such country wayside stations were so much a part of the scene and we are a lot poorer for their passing. 17 July 1967.

Left above: Shap Cutting (2): Only a couple of weeks before being withdrawn from service and about a quarter of an hour after 45072 had passed on the Morecambe, 'Britannia' 70038 *Robin Hood* followed with 1M38 1400 Glasgow Central-Manchester Victoria/Liverpool Exchange. This train divided at Preston. I do recall here I met a fellow photographer who did not take the picture because he felt the pylon rather spoilt the view; it was, he thought, a modern intrusion into the character of Shap Fell. Perhaps he was correct but it was a part of the overall scene and I thought it was well worth clicking the shutter. 22 July 1967.

Left below: Shap Summit: The view looking north at Shap Summit (916 feet above sea level, no doubt someone somewhere will translate that in to the unwanted metres). Heading south is '9F' 92212 with 5M27 0825 Larbert to Wallerscote Sidings (Northwich), the return empties of another block train still entrusted to steam at the time, the outward run conveying ICI Soda Ash. It is quite surprising to learn that the '9Fs' only worked over this part of the West Coast Main Line for the last two years of their lives; one wonders what service they could have given if they had been handed the chance. Shap Summit Signal Box is behind the train at the end of the cutting. 22 July 1967.

Shap Station (2): An almost Western Region scene at Shap Station as 'Standard 4' 75030 still in Western Region lined green livery ambles under the footbridge heading south with a short local ballast train for Tebay, complete with an ex-Great Western 'TOAD' brake van a long way from home. Just to add to the Western theme, at this precise time an elderly lady was testing the capabilities of the station porter to the limit by trying to book a mid-week return to Totnes in rural South Devon! I was able to offer some professional assistance. 17 July 1967.

Right above: Thrimby Grange (1): A real blast from the past at Thrimby Grange where the up main and up loop starting signals were ex-LNWR lower quadrants, replaced by the British Railways upper quadrant version very soon after this picture was taken. In complete contrast, the down starting signal opposite the signal box is much more modern for the era being a colour light! Going well on the 1 in 125 gradient, and passing these vintage signals in some style, is '9F' 92071 with the morning Carlisle to Crewe Basford Hall fully-fitted freight; the approach to Shap from the north is more gentle and banking assistance was rarely provided from Penrith for up trains. 22 July 1967.

Right below: Thrimby Grange (2): Not all railway photographers bothered with what we call the 'going away' shot, quite often they not only gave one an extra picture, they could portray a very different scene and be full of interest in their own right. Here are a couple of 'going away' shots at Thrimby Grange: the first being of 92071, seen in the previous picture passing the vintage signals and now about to pass the very large, and still open, limestone works built in the Second World War. Looking south the easier ascent to Shap Summit for trains from the north is very noticeable. 22 July 1967.

Thrimby Grange (3): I did not actually manage an approaching shot of this train, so for this one this is it! Immediately north of Thrimby Grange '9F' 92017 heads for Carlisle with a down freight from Crewe; the railway here running alongside the infant River Leith seen to the left and the sheep are grazing in the lush fields. The line has left behind the bleakness of the Westmorland Fells and dropped down to the pastoral charm of the Eden Valley. 22 July 1967.

Right above: Thrimby Grange (4): Despite the title *Steam North West* I have included just one diesel hauled train in its own right as the subject matter is very rare, and to many just as interesting as the passing steam age. The Class 28 Metrovick diesels as they were known were discussed in our look at Carnforth Shed and photographs of them working passenger trains are quite rare. Here D5702 is seen struggling with its six-coach load, mostly of elderly LMS stock, on the 1 in 125 ascent of Shap from the north at Thrimby Grange with another curious Summer Saturday train, 1M54 0900 Newcastle to Blackpool North. This ran in the peak season 8 July to 26 August, and was almost unique in being routed from Newcastle over the line through Hexham to Carlisle to continue south on the West Coast Main Line. D5702 was withdrawn in September 1968, one just one month after the end of the steam which it was supposed to replace. 22 July 1967.

Right below: Clifton & Lowther (1): In the cutting just to the north of the former Clifton & Lowther Station 'Black 5' 44674 heads north at 0950 with the first of the day's Summer Saturday extras, the 1S40 0825 Morecambe Promenade to Glasgow Central. No doubt after a hearty breakfast in their hotels or boarding houses, the holiday makers are returning home to the daily toil of city life in central Scotland. This train ran in the high peak 1 July to 19 August calling at Bare Lane and Carnforth which it departed at 0845. Except to pick up a banker at Tebay for the climb to Shap Summit, the train was advertised as running non-stop to Carlisle which it reached at 1017. After calling at Motherwell, the train arrived at Glasgow Central at 1250. Departing at 1326 the return working this day has already been featured coming out of Shap Cutting on its way south. This was the first picture taken on a memorable day of steam photography between here and Tebay. 22 July 1967.

Clifton & Lowther (4): With Penrith Beacon for a backdrop and in the pastoral setting of the lush countryside to the south of Penrith, 'Britannia' 70029 *Shooting Star* rounds the curve from the former Eden Valley Junction to Clifton & Lowther with 3K16 0655 Carlisle to Crewe parcels in rather fine style. Another bonus picture, taken just after 1000, this train is running about two hours late! This particular service was nicknamed and known to many as 'The Horse and Carriage' from the age when it was used to convey real horses and carriages for the landed gentry, in particular when the nobility returned from Bonnie Scotland. There is evidence of track renewal activity in the area at this time. 22 July 1967.

Left above: Clifton & Lowther (2): The view from the road bridge seen immediately behind 44674 heading 1S40 in the previous picture as another 'Black 5' 44985 heads north on a freight for Carlisle through the former Clifton & Lowther Station. This station was an early casualty closing to passengers on 4 July 1938 and completely on 1 June 1951. The former station buildings were still in evidence at the time behind the train with the signal box to the far left. 22 July 1967.

Left below: Clifton & Lowther (3): A view looking north, the previous picture was taken looking south from the road bridge under which '9F' 92071 has just emerged with a morning freight from Carlisle. The train has been routed into the up loop (which looks a little rusty) so that a faster southbound train could overtake; this proved to be a blessing for the photographers as we were able to head on to Thrimby Grange at a fairly fast pace and intercept it again and take that memorable shot of 92071 passing the LNWR lower quadrant signals. Lady Luck does shine sometimes. 22 July 1967.

Keswick: Penrith was the station for Ullswater; it was also once a Junction for the line which ran to Keswick which closed 6 March 1972. The line beyond Keswick through Bassenthwaite Lake and Cockermouth to Workington had closed from 18 April 1966. I only went to Keswick in diesel days, so I have included this rather fine shot from my collection. A timeless scene as 'Ivatt' 46432 arrives at Keswick with a train from Whitehaven and Workington to Penrith in July 1965. This engine spent seven years based at Workington Shed (12D) for such duties, and was withdrawn from Springs Branch, Wigan, in May 1967. Keswick is another of those places where a rail link would be very useful, and one can only wonder what an attraction a heritage railway on to Cockermouth would have been. July 1965.

Left above: Penrith for Ullswater (1): It was a long way from Plymouth to the far North West for the 100E, I remember on the Tuesday we had to call in at Penrith and leave the little car in a garage for the morning as it had developed a fault and objected to taking us any further for photography. Time then to spend on Penrith Station where we see 'Britannia' 70011 *Hotspur* rolling in with a southbound goods from Carlisle, passing the rather grand water tank and the lofty Penrith No 3 Signal Box. 18 July 1967.

Left below: Penrith for Ullswater (2): The 'going away' view of 70011 looking south towards Preston and included to show in particular the co-acting arm signal, once such a fairly common feature throughout the system, but few survive today. The lower arm is in the correct place, but for an approaching driver visibility of it is restricted, in this case by the station buildings. The top arm is a repeater which the driver can see from a much greater distance. Penrith No. 2 (The Yard) Signal Box is to the right and one can appreciate from this picture the long, gentle, left hand, northbound curve on which the station is situated. 18 July 1967.

Carlisle (1): Welcome to the Border City and the end of our journey from Crewe, with a few deviations on the way. I hope you the reader have enjoyed our nostalgic trip along the line. My first visit to Carlisle Station was on a dull and dismal June day in 1966 on the way home from Scotland, alighting from 1M37 1110 Perth-Birmingham New Street with Class 47 Diesel D1842 (now preserved as 47 192) on the left. To the right Ivatt Tank 41217 simmers away on station pilot duties. 24 June 1966.

Right above: Carlisle (2): Looking south at Carlisle Citadel Station as 41217 simmers in Bay 6, which is now used for the Settle and Carlisle Line Sprinter services. The high wall adjacent to the locomotive is the station wall, which until the very early 1950s supported the overall station roof. The buildings in the background were the former LNWR Crown Street Goods Depot which were closed *c.* February 1966 and demolished in the early 1970s, yet another victim of the abandonment by British Rail of general merchandise traffic. 24 June 1966.

Right below: Carlisle (3): Night Mail. A truly evocative and busy scene as 'Black 5' 44802 rests between duties alongside one of the most romantic of all trains, the up special TPO (Travelling Post Office) 1M44 1905 Glasgow Central to London Euston. This is the train which had already won everlasting fame for all the wrong reasons being the subject of the Great Train Robbery near Cheddington, Bucks, on 8 August 1963. The down working was also immortalised in the legendary film *Night Mail* made in 1936 by the GPO Film Unit. The clock shows 2112 so the train is on time, booked Carlisle 2105-2120. The streaky light to the left is the lamp of the Carriage & Wagon Examiner who would not stand still for the necessary sixty-second time exposure. 14 December 1967.

Carlisle (4): The old and the new by night: A truly nostalgic picture not only for devotees of steam, but one for the diesel enthusiasts as well. Class 45 'Peak' D12, later 45 011, stands at Platform 4 with 1N63 1605 Glasgow Central to Leeds City booked away from Carlisle at 1841, the timetable indicated that this train conveyed a 'Counter Buffet Bar with light refreshments, drinks and hot dishes to order.' One can only imagine the sheer delight of going to the bar, ordering a meal and enjoying both whilst the train climbed up through Mallerstang in the cold night air. 'Black 5' 44910 stands alongside in 'C' siding which was used for locomotives waiting to replace incoming locomotives from Scotland to work south. Note the ex-LNWR ground level, yellow, shunting signal in the foreground; a rare survivor even for 1967. 14 December 1967.

Right above: Carlisle (5): The glow of steam. D12 has departed on its journey south over the Settle & Carlisle line leaving a clear view from Platform 4 of 'Black 5' 44910 simmering away under the south footbridge, which is still in use and is now the only bridge to link the main part of the station to the island part. There is steam coming out everywhere it should, and probably where it should not; the cab is lit by the red glow from the firebox, and it all makes for a truly nostalgic memory of steam in the night. The station was opened on 1 September 1847 and probably steam had been there every night ever since. However, within two weeks it would be no more as steam finished at the Border City on the last day of 1967. 14 December 1967.

Right below: Carlisle (6): 44802 and the station lights make a good combination for a picture as the engine poses between shunting duties. Like Crewe, and indeed many other stations all over the system, night-time brought the mails, the parcels and the goods trains which ran while the nation slept. All manner of vans were attached, detached, shunted or transferred to another train and at night with steam, it was all a hustle and bustle which can never be recreated. The crossovers in the middle of Carlisle Station were controlled by Carlisle 4A Signal Box (which I talked my way into three years later) which was, unusually, on the upper floor of the main building with a bay window, and is just out of sight to the left of the picture. Note the BR ground disc shunting signal as opposed to the former LNWR type still in use as seen at the south end of the station. Manual signalling disappeared when Carlisle Power Signal Box opened in 1973, but if one knows where to look, the bay window for the former 4A is still there. 14 December 1967.

Carlisle (7): In the bleak mid-winter: Time to step out from the cover of the station roof and stand in the cold and the drizzle to see 44802, the engine glowing well in the night air with that lovely warming glow in the cab. Although this is just a shunting move, the engine is standing ready as if to head south either over Shap or the Settle & Carlisle, but not much more in the

way of steam would be heading away in any direction from the Border City for much longer. Of interest to the left is the DMU, one of the original Derby lightweight 79XXX sets with the yellow diamond control system and very few of these were ever painted blue. 14 December 1967.

Carlisle (8): Steam Beer: We conclude our very evocative look at 'Steam in the Night' as it came to an end in the Border City with another time exposure of sixty seconds at F8; the 'ghost figure' being the station shunter who would, of course, not stand still for the required minute. Now here is something different: I had already purchased a dozen bottles of Carlisle Brewery Beer, always noted for its creamy head and superb taste and, back in 1967, this brewery was still state owned (until 1973) under Lloyd George's State Management Scheme of 1916 (civil servants paid to brew and distribute beer is probably the best use ever found for them). When 44802 came in to the platform shortly after this picture was taken, the driver very kindly opened the injectors filling my rather large travelling bag with steam and making sure the twelve securely packed bottles got a good dousing. Thus at the Boxing Day slide show held at my late parents' house, those present were able to drink a toast to steam with genuine steam beer! 14 December 1967.

The Settle and Carlisle Railway—A Brief Glimpse

Garsdale water troughs: My visits to the Settle and Carlisle line were regrettably hindered by unfavourable weather, thus I do not have many quality pictures of the line in the BR Steam era, and mind you I have not got that many since! On a gloomy December day, an unidentified '9F' heads south with loaded coal passing over Garsdale water troughs, the highest in the world and laid out on one of the few level pieces of track to be found on this section of the line. The Garsdale down distant signal is to the left. I have included this picture despite the lack of decent weather as not many views seem to have been taken at this location as it was a long trek out from the station. 14 December 1967.

Arten Gill Viaduct (2): Life changing. A closer view of the splendid eleven arched, 117 feet high Arten Gill Viaduct after which our house is named. An unidentified '9F' is pictured heading north amid some rather nice autumn colours with a train of mainly coal. It was after taking this picture I decided to descend to the valley floor to find the road back to Dent Station. Unfortunately I lost my ground and fell about 60 feet down the bank, my left leg hitting a rock almost as I came to a halt and I was unable to move for some time. To cut a long story short, the leg never fully healed, and ever since I have had a slight limp and now and again some pain, but the camera and the film were safe! 26 October 1967.

Left above: Dent: The highest main line station in England at 1,150 feet above sea level and over four miles from the village it purports to serve; this is a remote spot. Closed in 1970, the station re-opened in 1986. Today the buildings are in private ownership and are used for holiday accommodation, a great place to spend a few days. An unidentified 'Black 5' is seen heading south with 7P68 1310 Carlisle Yard to Skipton freight in the declining afternoon light. 26 October 1967.

Left below: Arten Gill Viaduct (1): The railway runs high above beautiful Dent Dale for a couple of miles on Stonehouse Brow, a ledge carved into the slopes of Great Knoutberry Hill. I had alighted from a train at Dent Station and a kindly shepherd, who I met by chance, took me out alongside the line; not a recognised footpath hence this unusual long distance view of a north bound freight train crossing Arten Gill Viaduct. The viaduct is named after the fast running beck it traverses. With Wold Fell (maximum height 1,834 feet) behind, and to the top right the spoil heaps of material excavated from the nearby cuttings; a plume of steam in the right place, beautiful scenery and a touch of autumn sunshine make a good combination. 26 October 1967.

Approaching Blea Moor: A picture not quite of the high standard and lighting quality expected but included as it depicts a very rare visitor to the Settle & Carlisle Line, former Western Region 7029 *Clun Castle* (it was built after nationalisation so was not a true Great Western specimen) working 1F50 0835 Kings Cross-Carlisle the rather grandly named 'Splendour of Steam' rail tour run by the A4 Preservation Society, the 'Castle' having taken over at Peterborough. 7029 had by this time been purchased for preservation, and (as far as I know) was the first of the class to be seen here, but not the first to be seen at Carlisle as 5000 *Launceston Castle* was borrowed by the LMS in 1926 for trials on the West Coast Main Line. Not unusually, the strong westerly wind is blowing from Chapel-le-Dale and the smoke from the hard working engine is obscuring the view of Pen-y-ghent. Ribblehead Viaduct is behind the train and the easterly slope of Park Fell is to the right. My trip to get here was: early turn at Saltash booking office; then late Friday afternoon train Plymouth to Paddington; Euston to Carlisle sleeper; 2P69 0835 DMU Carlisle-Skipton alighting at Ribblehead at 1026 with a bag well-stocked with mother's sandwiches, a day etched in the memory. Many others will remember this as the day BBC Radio One started broadcasting, but due to the technology of the day we did hear much from Tony Blackburn and company on the wind swept fells. 30 September 1967.

Ribblehead, the loo with a view: Having arrived at Ribblehead after the long trek from Plymouth just described, the Station Inn was a welcome sight especially for a warm drink and to take care of one's physical needs. I hope nobody will be offended by relating this incident: it was while using the pub toilet that I heard a whistle and the sound of a steam hauled northbound freight approaching, so the only thing for it was to grab the camera and throw open the toilet window and take my first ever view of Ribblehead Viaduct. As it turned out, quite a view from the loo with the neat and tidy pub garden in the foreground, the great structure itself seen in its setting of the crossing of Batty Moss where Ribblesdale meets Chapel-le-Dale and, dominating the background, the great hill of Whernside, which at 2,415 feet is the highest point in the County of North Yorkshire. It was in the pub that one of the locals informed me of the local legend regarding the Ribblehead weather, 'if you can't see the hills it is raining, if you can see the hills it is about to rain.' Well it did not rain that day, the sun did not shine for much of it, but that strong westerly wind certainly made its presence felt. 30 September 1967.

Horton-in-Ribblesdale (1): Looking south from the rear of 2L69 1145 Skipton to Carlisle DMU at 1225 and the sun is just bursting out after a shower of rain to give some dramatic lighting conditions, and in particular highlighting the steam from the '9F' heading a down northbound freight which has been halted and then reversed onto the up line for my train to pass—standard former Midland Railway operation. Having alighted from the train an elderly lady carrying the morning's shopping from Settle is heading for the station exit and home; probably not taking a blind bit of notice of the steam engine, after all they would be there forever. Well in just two months regular steam through here would finish. 26 October 1967.

Left above: Ribblehead Viaduct looking north: Much has been written elsewhere about what is probably the most iconic image of the Settle and Carlisle line; Ribblehead Viaduct. At 440 yards in length, a maximum height of 104 feet and consisting of twenty-four arches, every sixth pier is of extra strength so in the unlikely event of one arch falling only five would follow. A morning view from Batty Moss as a lengthy up freight formed of open wagons heads south with Whernside mostly hidden by cloud. The viaduct suffered damage due to the wind and the rain and this was used as the excuse for a closure proposal in the 1980s of the whole line, fortunately common sense prevailed and the viaduct was repaired and the line reprieved. 30 September 1967.

Left below: Ribblehead Viaduct looking south: A lucky burst of sunshine as an unidentified 'Black 5' heads away from Blea Moor and onto the viaduct with a southbound mixed goods train. Park Fell, with an elevation of 1,847 feet and partly hidden by cloud, is not perhaps as impressive as Whernside but it is still an imposing backdrop. There is the first tint of autumn colour, yet Batty Moss in the shadow of the viaduct is still green and pleasant. The Station Inn mentioned earlier is just out of sight to the far left background. 30 September 1967.

POP. 700

ALTITUDE 850 FT.

HORTON-IN-RIBBLESDALE

YOU ARE NOW IN

YORK-SHIRE

WEST RIDING

AUDI CONSILIUM

HORTON IN RIBBLESDALE

Horton-in-Ribblesdale (2): Just seven miles from Settle Junction which we visited in our journey from Carnforth over the 'Little' North Western route we complete our journey south and briefly glimpse the Settle and Carlisle line at Horton-in-Ribblesdale. A pause to take a look at a piece of the station infrastructure, the rather decorative and informative station information board, with the background setting of Pen-y-ghent (2,277 feet in elevation,) and unlike at Ribblehead four weeks earlier, not a cloud to block the view. I wonder if the particularly accurate population count has altered much over the years. 26 October 1967.

August 1968
The End of Steam on British Rail

To mark the forty-fifth anniversary of the End of Steam on British Rail, a few recollections of those first two weekends in August 1968 as the age of steam finally passed in to history.

Carnforth Shed (1): Most people think of the end of steam as going out in a blaze of glory with rail tours going here, there and everywhere in the North West on the first Sunday of that month, some of which I have covered in our journeys around the area, and the famous '15 Guinea Special' which was the last one of all. There was another side to the story as the remaining steam engines were brought back to their sheds for the last time, fires were dropped and they joined the ever increasing long lines of stored locomotives whose work was done for ever; rust and dirt now was the order of the day. Already earmarked for preservation are maroon Ivatt Mogul 46441 and a Fairburn tank. In the background Kier Sidings is full of withdrawn locomotives with some newly arrived from their last duties still emitting those final exhausts. A Class 40 diesel and a Class 28 'Metrovick' are stabled on the fuelling point and to the right are wagons of coal that will probably be surplus to requirements. Crag Bank Hill a local landmark dominates the background. 2 August 1968.

Carnforth Shed (2): This visit to Carnforth Shed was organised by the RCTS of which I have been a member for over fifty years. Participants were allowed to park their cars by Kier Sidings. Interesting to note the car with its door open parked alongside 'Black 5' 44894, still emitting a few last breaths of steam, is an Austin 1100 with a top speed of 76 mph and would have been just over a year old. It bears an 'F' suffix to the number plate, annual suffixes changed on the first of August and in 1967 that was indeed 'F,' the first year the new registrations were transferred from January to August. Not many motorists had the chance to take their fairly new car on to a coal encrusted steam shed. I wonder if the proud owner will recognise his car. 2 August 1968.

Carnforth Shed (3): The last of the '9Fs.' There was no great fanfare or last special rail tour for this class to bow out in glory. The last two working '9F's' were this pair, 92160 nearest the camera parked chimney to chimney with 92167. The former was observed running light engine at Skipton on 13 June 1968, the last known sighting of a '9F' in service. 92167 was observed at Carnforth on 8 June having returned from Neville Hill (Leeds) with its rear driving coupling rods disconnected after problems encountered whilst working the return empty oil tanks to Heysham. Both engines were laid up because of their deplorable condition, an inglorious end for a powerful and successful class of 251 locomotives introduced as late as 1954. 2 August 1968.

Lostock Hall (3): Coal that will probably be never used for the purpose it was intended; I wonder how much of it ended up in the hearths of the local railwaymen? '8F' 48765 is still in steam as she joins in what is in outward appearance a fairly smart line of working engines but what is in reality another queue of now unwanted motive power, for it had been decreed by the powers that be this was now a diesel (and in some cases electric) only railway; yet another aspect to August 1968. However, it was not all gloom and doom that weekend. 3 August 1968.

Left above: Lostock Hall (1): A gathering of steam: The following day and the very sad scene at Lostock Hall Shed, engines everywhere and hardly one in steam, the slaughter was just about complete. Lines of locomotives in various states of repair or in some cases disrepair all lined up in some sort of final melancholy salute to steam. The scrap merchants were probably rubbing their hands with glee. For my part and many others this was the real face of the end of steam, where the era concluded in a sea of rust, grime and dirt; there would be no big final salute for these once and in most cases fairly recent work horses of the rails. It was sad, yet I feel a privilege to witness scenes like this. I will let the picture speak for itself. 3 August 1968.

Left below: Lostock Hall (2): Steam for scrap: On one of the two sidings which once led to the former L & Y Lostock Hall carriage shed situated beside the West Coast Main Line at Croston Road, and adjacent to the still extant double track line which connects Farington Junction with Lostock Hall Junction. A rather sad looking batch of locomotives with a 43XXX Ivatt Mogul at the head await that final journey to the breakers yard; yet another image which symbolises the end of steam, it was not all rail tours and fine last runs, it was in most cases dereliction and decay. 3 August 1968

Copy Pit: The following day saw a number of rail tours run by various organisations to mark the end of steam, some of which have already been documented on the various lines visited in our travels around North West England. All the trains were well filled and many people turned out to witness the occasion. A good crowd has assembled as 'Black 5s' 44874 + 45017 forge past the distant signal for Copy Pit Signal Box with 1Z79 Stephenson Locomotive Society (Midland Area) 'Farewell to Steam No. 2' as they make a fine ascent of the bank, we have already seen this train at Huncoat. This is indeed a picture which captures the atmosphere of the day. After this penultimate weekend of steam, there was just one further grand occasion to come. 4 August 1968.

Parkside: So it all came to an end with the running of 1T57, the '15 Guinea Special' from Liverpool to Carlisle by way of Manchester, Blackburn, Hellifield and the Settle route, the very last steam hauled train to be run by British Rail. The first leg from Liverpool Lime Street to Manchester Victoria was hauled by 'Black 5' 45110 seen here approaching Parkside. The train has just passed under the M6 motorway (no three lanes each way of bumper to bumper traffic back then) with the rear of the train still passing over the west junction of Lowton Junction, the tall home signal clearly visible, a triangular junction that was once the original route of the West Coast Main Line and now electrified for diversions. Through the left hand motorway arch the home signal protecting the branch from Parkside Colliery can be spotted. Newton-le-Willows Signal Box can just be glimpsed under the right hand motorway arch, and the chimneys and cooling towers in the background denote the former Bold Power Station. A much changed scene nowadays, but back to 1968 as 1T57 is about to make a special stop as we are in the cradle where it all began in the North West. 11 August 1968.

Ribblehead: For the leg from Manchester Victoria to Carlisle 1T57 was hauled by the last remaining 'Pacific' 70013 *Oliver Cromwell* seen here forging north and crossing Ribblehead Viaduct in a rare burst of sun with Pen-y-ghent for once clearly visible and dominating the skyline behind the train. On this day I saw possibly the most people I have ever seen in this isolated spot; it has to be remembered we were all here to witness a piece of history. 11 August 1968.

Left above: Parkside the Huskisson Memorial (1): This is where it all began, the Liverpool & Manchester Railway opened on 15 September 1830, the first double track intercity passenger main line in the world where all the trains ran to a timetable. The celebrations of the opening day were somewhat over-shadowed by the death of William Huskisson, the popular Member of Parliament for Liverpool. He alighted from a train during the water stop here at Parkside and was hit by none other than the famous *Rocket* passing in the other direction, which went over Huskisson's leg and the unfortunate gentleman died from his injuries later the same day. A memorial to Huskisson was erected at the spot in 1831 and still stands to this day, very appropriate that the last steam train of all should commemorate where indeed it had all began. 11 August 1968.

Left below: Parkside the Huskisson Memorial (2): 45110 seen during the stop to commemorate William Huskisson, the actual memorial is the white building to the right and the view is looking towards Manchester. It is a pity that vegetation today rather obscures the memorial. Notable in both pictures of this occasion are the number of passengers and spectators seemingly roaming around at will on a main line, even ladders had been provided for access to and from the special train. I cannot see Network Rail (as is today) allowing the world and his wife to wander about the railway, but back in 1968 a thing called common sense prevailed. A study of the people in both pictures is a great statement of late sixties fashion! 11 August 1968.

Arten Gill: High arches in Dent Dale. A fitting location to record the two 'Black 5s' 44871 + 44781 entrusted with the return leg of 1T57 from Carlisle to Manchester Victoria by the same route. The light may not have been as kind in Dent Dale as one would have liked, but at least it was not raining and it was a rather special occasion. I must point out great care was taken during the descent from Arten Gill after the picture was taken, I did not want an action reply of what had happened on the opposite bank the previous October, but there was no time to waste. 11 August 1968.

Ribblehead (1): Very fortunately, 1T57 was booked to take a twenty-minute stop for water at Blea Moor which gave one the chance of a shot in Dent Dale and hopefully a chase to get another at Ribblehead, which was successfully accomplished, but only just! The two 'Black 5s' were captured again as they head south coming off Ribblehead Viaduct and away into history with the sun in and out and a very bleak looking Blea Moor behind. So it thus was the end of steam, well not quite. 11 August 1968.

Ribblehead (2): In the glow of a Pennine Storm: We knew 70013 which had worked the outward part of 1T57 would be returning light engine about forty-five minutes after the return leg worked by the two 'Black 5s' seen in the picture at the top of the page. Most of the chasing camera pack dashed off to Liverpool for the last rites, but we remained for that last light engine and in the intervening gap the clouds gathered as they do in this part of the world. As 70013 came into view fate took a hand and a ray of sun shone on the Pacific with Whernside looking very foreboding behind. My very last shot of working steam on British Rail, and indeed one the best ever taken. A classic shot for a classic moment, and with that I sign off. 11 August 1968.